The Kitchen Table Recipe Book

Written & Illustrated by
Lloie Schwartz

D1511931

illustrations: Lloie Schwartz
book design: Meg Swansen
logo design: Elizabeth Zimmermann

For additional copies of this book,
please join us for breakfast or lunch at the
Kitchen Table
118 E Third Street
Marshfield, WI 54449
(715) 387-2601

or call
Schoolhouse Press
6899 Cary Bluff
Pittsville, WI 54466
(715) 884-2799

ISBN: 0-942018-24-9
Library of Congress Control Number: 2003116560

Acknowledgements:
Thank you to my sister Meg without whom this book would
not be. Thank you to all my dear devoted customers for
insisting on a new book. Thank you to all my teachers.

... OF CONTENTS:

Preface:

These are only recipes; anyone can read them. What you bring to them in the way of experience will determine the outcome.

Like everything else, cooking requires practice, practice, practice - and as you practice, mistakes will occur; some good, some not. Remember, most recipes come into being through mistakes and experiments. Contrary to your childhood training, I encourage you to play with your food:

- try new ideas
- change ingredients
- experiment with seasonings
- be creative and innovative
- get outside the recipe or the box
- get excited

I have discovered that when working with food there are so many variables, precisely determining the outcome is not possible. That's what makes cooking an adventure and a challenge.

Preparing food I like and sharing it with others is a gift I give myself as it brings me great joy and satisfaction.

That's why I own a restaurant, so I can make my living playing with food.

BEAUTIFUL

SOUP

White Chili - yield 3 gallons

4 onions diced
3 T butter
4 qts water
1/4 c turkey or chicken soup base
4 Tbl dry basil
1/2 t ground cloves
2 Tbl chili powder
3 Tbl ground cumin
1 Tbl ground coriander
1 1/2 t granulated garlic
1 lg (26 oz) can chopped green chilies
1 - 4oz can diced jalapeños
4 c salsa
1 bunch cilantro chopped
juice from 2 limes
1 #10 (102 oz) can white beans
4 lbs cooked turkey or chicken cubed
1 - 14oz bag tortilla chips crushed

Brown onions in butter. Add water and seasonings. Now add green chilies, jalapeños, salsa, lime juice, and chopped cilantro. Bring to a boil, turn down and simmer 5 min. Remove from heat and stir in white beans, tortilla chips and cubed turkey. Taste, then distribute into containers and chill overnight.

Potato Leek Soup - yield 3 gallons

2-3 Tbl butter
4-5 lbs leeks washed and sliced in 1" pieces
10 lbs potatoes peeled and sliced
6 qts water
1 c chicken soup base
1 t pepper
1Tbl sugar
1 bunch parsley. Tops and stems chopped separately

Lightly brown leeks in butter. Add water and seasonings and bring to a boil. Add potatoes and chopped stems of parsley. Bring back to a boil and cook until potatoes are just barely tender, about 5 min.. Remove from heat and add chopped parsley tops. Distribute immediately into containers to cool.

For regular potato soup substitute 4-5 chopped onions.

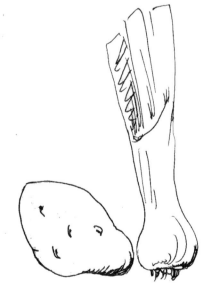

<u>Hungarian</u> <u>Goulash</u> <u>Soup</u> - yield 3 gallons

First make beef stew meat on page on pg 51
and simmer 2-3 hours.
4 onions diced
3 Tbl butter
4 Tbl paprika
3 Tbl ground caraway seed
1/2 c beef soup base
6 qts water
1 pkg kluski noodles cooked
or cooked dumplings pg 29

Roux: 1 cup flour & 1 cup butter
cook for 10 min. and set aside

Brown onions in butter. Add water, cooked stew meat with
liquid, seasonings and bring up to a boil. Turn down and
add cooked roux stirring vigorously. Remove from heat and
add cooked noodles.

If you just want to have
Hungarian goulash, omit the
water and soup base and
serve over wide noodles.

Caraway

Hamburger Dumpling Soup - yield 3 gallons

5 lbs hamburger
1 c flour
3 T butter
3 lg onions diced
2 lbs carrots sliced
1 bunch celery sliced
2 green peppers diced
1 #10 can (102 oz) can diced tomatoes
1 16 oz can tomato paste (2 cups)
4 Tbl basil
2 Tbl dill weed
4 Tbl sugar
1 t granulated garlic
2 t pepper
1 cup beef soup base
6 qts water
3 c burgundy

Brown the hamburger, drain and stir in 1 cup flour. Set aside. Brown onions in 3 T butter. Add veggies and sauté 5 min. Add water, tomatoes, tomato paste, seasonings, soup base and bring to a boil. Turn down and simmer for about 8 min. Now add cooked hamburger, cooked dumplings and Burgundy. Remove from heat and taste.

Dumplings:
7 eggs
2 c flour
1 t salt

Mix in a small bowl with a fork. Cook in 4 qts boiling salted water. Make by using a teaspoon or a dumpling maker. Drain and add to soup at the end.

<u>French</u> <u>Onion</u> <u>Soup</u> <u>w/</u> <u>Croutons</u> - yield 2 gallons

8-10 large yellow onions, sliced (1 gallon)
4 Tbl butter
1 c beef soup base
1 t granulated garlic
1 Tbl sugar
1 t pepper
2 c dry onions
2 c white wine (chablis)

Peel and slice onions. Sauté them in butter over low to medium heat for about 1 hour or until brown and caramelized. Then add water, seasonings and dry onions and bring to a boil. Turn down and simmer 20 min.

Remove from heat and add white wine. Serve with croutons and shredded swiss cheese.

<u>Croutons:</u>
6 qts cubed stale bread
1 lb melted butter
1 t granulated garlic
1 Tbl dill weed (dry)

Mix melted butter with garlic and dill. Put bread cubes on the grill and pour butter mixture over them. Keep tossing until all are buttered. Then fry, turning often until golden brown and crisp.

Fisherman's Chowder - yield 3 gallons

5 lbs cod cut in chunks
2 Tbl bacon fat
1/2 c crumbled bacon
4-5 onions diced
2 green peppers diced
1 #10 can (102 oz) diced tomatoes
1 bottle ketchup - 14 oz
3 c salsa - med hot
5 qts water
2-3 bay leaves
2 Tbl salt
2 t sugar
2 t pepper
1 t Italian herbs
1/2 t cayenne pepper
2 t granulated garlic
1 bunch parlsey with stems chopped
10 c cubed potatoes - fresh or frozen

Pre-cook cod for 5 min in simmering salted water. Drain and set aside. Brown onions in bacon fat. Add green peppers and cook 3 min. Now add everything **except** cod and bring to a boil. Turn down to simmer until potatoes are done, about 3-4 min. Remove from heat and add cooked cod and crumbled bacon. Divide up into containers immediately and chill.

<u>Cream</u> <u>of</u> <u>Broccoli</u> <u>Soup</u> - yield 3 gallons

8-9 broccoli crowns
2 onions diced
6 qts water
1 c chicken soup base
1/2 t dry tarragon
1/3 c lemon juice concentrate
1 t pepper
1 qt heavy cream
Roux = 2 c butter & 2 c flour

Make roux by cooking butter and flour together for 10 min and set aside.
Cut flowers off broccoli crowns and set aside. Chop stems in food processor and set aside. Saute onions in butter. Add water and seasonings and bring to a boil. Add processed broccoli stems and return to a boil and cook a few minutes. Last add broccoli flowers and hot roux stirring until thickened. Remove from heat and add heavy cream. Immediately divide soup into containers to cool.

<u>Corn</u> <u>Chowder</u> - yield 3 gallons

3 lg onions diced
3 T butter
1 bunch celery sliced
6 quarts water
3 Tbl sugar
1 c chicken soup base
1 t pepper
5 lbs corn kernels - fresh or frozen
8 c diced frozen hashbrowns
1 can (26 oz) diced green chilies
1 qt heavy cream
Roux:
2 c butter
2 c flour
Cook butter and flour together for 10 min and set aside.

Lightly brown onions in butter, then add celery and sauté a few minutes. Pour in water, add seasonings and bring to a boil. Next add corn and potatoes and return to a boil. Turn down heat and add hot roux. Stir until thickened and

remove from heat. Last add green chilies and cream. Divide up into containers immediately and chill.

<u>Kitchen</u> <u>Table</u> <u>Chili</u> - yield 6 gallons

10 lbs ground beef

8-10 lg onions
5 green peppers   >>>put through food processor
2 bunches celery

1 - 4oz cans diced jalapeños
1/2 cup red wine vinegar
2 - 12 oz cans beer
4 cups salsa
3 #10 cans (102 oz) small red beans
1 #10 can (102 oz) diced tomatoes
4 1/2 cups tomato paste

<u>Dry</u> <u>mix</u>

2 cups flour
1 1/4 cups taco mix
1/2 cup chili powder
2 t granulated garlic
1 t ground cloves
1 Tbl black pepper
1/2 cup ground cumin
3 Tbl ground coriander
1/2 cup basil
1/4 cup oregano
1/4 cup sugar
1/2 cup ham soup base

Brown beef. Add processed vegetables and cook 15 min. Stir in dry mix and remove from heat. Stir in remaining ingredients. Put in gallon containers and freeze.

.

Lou's **Mushroom** **Soup**- Yield 3 gallons

5 lbs. mushrooms sliced
3 onions diced
6 qts. water
1 c. beef soup base
1 t pepper
3 bay leaves
1 t ground rosemary
2 cups white wine
4 cups sour cream
roux = 3 c. butter, 3 c. flour

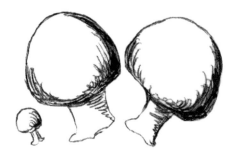

Make roux by cooking butter and flour together in a
separate pot for 10 min. Set aside.
Brown onions in some butter. Add mushrooms and sauté
until lightly brown.
Add water and seasonings. Bring to a boil, turn down and
simmer 5 min.
Stir in hot roux and remove from heat.
Cool overnight.
Before re-heating, add white wine and sour cream.

Potato - Cucumber Soup - Yield 3 gallons

3 onions diced
4 qts. water
10 lbs. potatoes peeled and sliced
10 - 12 cucumbers peeled, seeded & cubed
1 cup chicken soup base
3 Tbl. dill weed
1 t pepper
4 cups sour cream

Brown onions in some butter.
Add water and bring to a boil.
Add potatoes, seasonings and cucumbers.
Bring back to a boil. Turn down and simmer until potatoes are just cooked (about 5 min.).
Refrigerate overnight.
Before re-heating stir in sour cream.

Gazpacho with Croutons - yield 2 gallons

2 #10 (102 oz) cans diced
     tomatoes
1 1/2 cups tomato paste
2 qts. water
2 c salsa
1/2 cup olive oil
4 Tbl. sugar
4 Tbl. sweet basil
2 Tbl. dill weed
1 t granulated garlic
4 Tbl. beef soup base -
diluted in hot water

1 bunch parsley
2 green peppers
1 bunch celery
3-4 cucumbers peeled &
seeded
1 bunch green onions
juice from 1 lemon
1 t tabasco
1 Tbl. Worcestershire sauce
salt & pepper to taste

Run tomatoes and all vegetables through the food processor and chop coarsely. Combine with all the rest of the ingredients and chill overnight. Serve chilled with croutons.

CROUTONS

6 qts. cubed stale bread
1 lb. butter

1 Tbl. dill weed
1 t granulated garlic

Melt butter with dill and garlic. Pour over bread cubes and toss and fry until golden brown.

Cream Of Cauliflower Soup- yield 4 gallons

2 onions diced
2 lbs. carrots sliced
1 bunch celery sliced
6 qts. water
1 c. chicken soup base
1 t mixed herbs
2 bay leaves
1 t pepper
(1 t curry powder opt)
6 heads cauliflower cut bite size
2 Tbl. lemon juice
1 qt. heavy cream
1 bunch parsley, chopped
roux = 3 cups butter & 3 cups flour

Make roux by cooking butter and flour together for 10 min.
in a separate pot and set aside.
Sauté onions in some butter. Add carrots and celery and
cook about 5 min. or until vegetables are fragrant. Add
water, soup base and seasonings. Bring to a boil, add cauliflower and lemon juice. Bring back to a boil and cook 3-4
min. Then add hot roux. Cook & stir until thick and remove
from heat. Add heavy cream and chopped parsley.

<u>24</u> <u>Carrot</u> <u>Gold</u> <u>Soup</u> - yield 3 gallons

10 lbs. carrots
6 qts. water
1 1/2 qts orange juice
grated rind of 2 lg. oranges
3 t ground ginger
1/2 t cinnamon
3 Tbl. granulated onion
3 Tbl. brown sugar
1 c. chicken soup base
roux = 2 c. butter & 2 c. flour

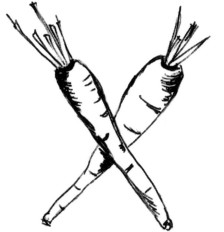

First make roux by cooking
butter and flour together for 10
min and set aside.
Bring 6 qts. water to a boil.
Slice 7 lbs. of the carrots and chop the other 3 lbs in the
food processor until fine. Add to boiling water.
Then add all the rest of the ingredients, **except** the roux.
Bring back to a boil, turn down and simmer until carrot
slices are tender (about 5 min.).
Last, stir in hot roux and simmer until thickened.

<u>Cuban</u> <u>Black</u> <u>Bean</u> <u>Soup</u>- yield 3 gallons

Soak 4 lbs. black turtle beans overnight
drain and add:
2 gals. water
1 t granulated garlic
3 bay leaves
1 c. blackstrap molasses
1/4 t cayenne pepper
1 t tabasco
1 t mixed herbs
1/2 c. ham soup base
1/2 c. beef soup base

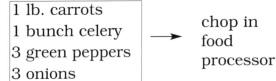

| 1 lb. carrots
1 bunch celery
3 green peppers
3 onions | → | chop in
food
processor |

2 1/2 lbs. ham cubed
roux = 1/2 c. bacon fat & 1/2 c. flour
4 c. cooked white rice

Make roux by cooking bacon fat and flour together for 5 min.
& set aside. Bring beans and water to a boil. Turn down and
add seasonings and molasses. Simmer 1 hour, then add
processed vegetables and cubed ham. Return to a boil, turn
down and simmer another 20 min. or until beans are
cooked. Stir in <u>hot</u> roux. Add rice just before serving.

16

Boston Clam Chowder - yield 4 gallons

1 c. crumbled bacon
2-3 Tbl. bacon fat
6 onions diced
2 - 51 oz. cans chopped sea clams
1 46 oz. can sea clam juice
5 lbs. diced potatoes
salt to taste
2 tsp. pepper
1 tsp. mixed herbs
1 Tbl. dill weed
2 t granulated garlic
1/4 t cayenne pepper
5 qts water
1 qt heavy cream
1 bunch parsley
roux = 3 c. butter & 3 c. flour

Make roux by cooking butter and flour together for 10 min. and set aside.

Sauté onions in bacon fat. Add water, clams & juice and bring to a boil. Add potatoes and seasonings and cook until potatoes are barely done. stir in hot roux. Cook until thickened and remove from heat and add heavy cream.

Last add chopped parsley and crumbled bacon.

Ham and Dumpling Soup - yield 4 gallons

3 Tbl bacon fat

4 onions diced

2 lbs. carrots sliced

1 bunch celery sliced

2 gals. water

1 c. chicken soup base

1 t pepper

1 Tbl. dill weed

3 Tbl. vinegar

3 lbs. cabbage cubed

3 lbs. ham, diced

Dumplings:

7 eggs	
2 c. flour	>>>stir together with a fork
1 t salt	

Brown onions in fat, then add carrots & celery and sauté 10 min. Add water and seasonings. Bring to a boil and cook 10 min. Make dumplings right into boiling soup by plopping in teaspoons-full of batter, or use dumpling-maker pictured above.

Last add ham & cabbage, bring back to a boil and simmer 5 min. Garnish with parsley.

Lentil Vegetable Soup - yield 3 1/2 gallons

2 Tbl butter
2 onions diced
2 lbs. carrots sliced
1 bunch celery sliced
1 green pepper diced
3 bay leaves
1 t granulated garlic
1 t pepper
3 Tbl. sugar
1/2 tsp. ground cloves
1 cup ham soup base
6 qts. water
1 #10 (102 oz.) can diced tomatoes
2 c. tomato paste
1/2 c. red wine vinegar
2 lbs. brown or red lentils

Brown onions in butter. Add carrots, celery and pepper.
Sauté about 10 min. stirring often.
Next add all the rest of the ingredients and bring to a boil.
Turn down and simmer 20 min. or until
lentils are tender.
Remove from heat.

19

<u>Garden</u> <u>Pea</u> <u>Soup</u> - yield 3 gallons-

3 Tbl. butter
2 onions diced
10 lbs. frozen peas - thawed
1/2 c. chopped fresh mint leaves
4 Tbl. sugar
1 t black pepper
1 cup chicken soup base
2 gals. water
roux = 1 1/2 c. butter & 1 1/2 c. flour

Make roux by cooking butter and flour together 10 min. and set aside.
Lightly sauté onions in butter.
Add peas and mint, cook until peas are tender, 15-20 min.
Set aside 1/4 of the peas and run the rest through the food processor.
Next put 2 gals. water in a large pot.
Add chicken base and sugar and bring to a boil.
Turn down and whisk in hot roux.
Then add pureéd pea mixture and the whole peas. Remove from heat and taste.

Cream of Potato Soup - yield 3 gallons

2 Tbl. butter
4 onions diced
10 lbs. potatoes peeled & sliced
1 t pepper
1 bunch parsley & stems
1 c. chicken soup base
6 qts. water
1 qt. heavy cream
roux = 2 c. butter & 2 c. flour

Make roux by cooking butter and
flour together for 10 min. and set aside.
Lightly brown onions in butter.
Add water and bring to a boil.
Add seasonings, potatoes and chopped stems of parsley.
Bring back to a boil and cook about 5 min. or until potatoes
are barely tender. Stir in hot roux until thickened.
Remove from heat and add heavy cream and chopped pars-
ley tops.

<u>Cream</u> <u>of</u> <u>Reuben</u> <u>Soup</u> - yield 3 gallons

3 Tbl. butter
4 onions diced
1 - 28 oz. can sauerkraut
6 qts. water
1 c. chicken soup base
2 Tbl. Poupon mustard
1 t horseradish
1 Tbl. dill weed
1 Tbl ground caraway seed
1 t granulated garlic
1 t pepper
1 Tbl. sugar
8 c. cooked diced corned beef
1 c parmesan/romano cheese
1 qt heavy cream
3-4 c shredded swiss for topping
roux = 3 c. butter & 3 c. flour

Make roux by cooking butter and flour together 10 min. and set aside.

Brown onions in butter. Cut up and add sauerkraut, water, seasonings and corned beef. Bring to a boil, turn down and simmer 5 min. Now add hot roux and parmesan stirring until thickened. Last add cream and remove from heat. Serve topped with swiss cheese.

<u>Cream</u> <u>of</u> <u>Spinach</u> <u>Soup</u> - yield 3 gallons

6 - 10 oz. pkgs. frozen chopped spinach, thawed
2 Tbl. butter
4 onions diced
3/4 c. chicken soup base
7 qts. water
1/2 t nutmeg
1 qt. heavy cream
roux = 3 c. butter & 3 c. flour

Make roux by cooking butter and
flour together for 10 min. Set aside.
Lightly brown onions.
Add thawed spinach and cook 10-15
min.
Pureé spinach in food processor until very fine.
Return mixture to soup pot and add water, soup base and
nutmeg.
Bring to a boil, turn down and whisk in hot roux. Remove
from heat and stir in heavy cream. Taste.

<u>Tomato</u> <u>Dill</u> <u>Soup</u> - yield 4 gallons

2 Tbl. butter
4 onions diced
2 qts. water
2 46 oz. cans tomato juice
2 #10 (102 oz.) cans diced tomatoes
4 1/2 c. tomato paste
2 1/2 c, honey
1/2 t tabasco
3 tsp. granulated garlic
1 c. beef soup base
1 t pepper
1/2 t cayenne pepper
2 Tbl. chili powder
2 Tbl. sweet basil
3 Tbl. dill weed

Brown onions in butter.
Put diced tomatoes through
food processor briefly so they are
a little smaller. Now add all ingredients except honey to the
pot and bring carefully to a boil stirring often. This soup
likes to stick and burn! Simmer 15 min. and remove from
heat. Stir in honey.
Garnish with a dollop of sour cream and chopped parsley.

Cream of Turkey & Wild Rice Soup - yield 3 gallons

3 Tbl. butter
2 onions diced
1 bunch celery sliced
8 qts. water
3/4 c. turkey soup base
1/4 c. chicken soup base
1 t Italian herbs
1 t pepper
1 qt. heavy cream
3 lbs. cubed cooked turkey
roux = 3 c. butter & 3 c. flour
2 qts. cooked wild rice blend

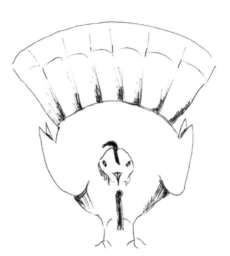

Make roux by cooking butter & flour together 10 min. Set
aside.
Brown onions in butter.
Add celery and sauté about 5 min.
Add water and seasonings and bring to a boil.
Add turkey and return to a boil.
Turn down and stir in hot roux. Continue cooking until
thickened, remove from heat and add heavy cream.
Just before serving, heat rice in microwave and add.

Fifteen Bean Soup -yield 4 gallons-

5 lbs. mixed or "calico" beans
6 qts. water
3/4 c. beef soup base
1/3 c. ham soup base
3 bay leaves
1 t granulated garlic
3 Tbl. ground cumin
1/2 t cayenne pepper
1 t black pepper
1 t tabasco
1/2 c. blackstrap molasses
1/2 c. honey
1 #10 (102 oz.) diced tomatoes

1 lb. carrots
1 bunch celery
3 onions
3 green peppers
3 Kielbasa sausages

→ put all vegetables and Kielbasa through the food processor

Soak beans overnight. Drain and rinse.
Put beans, water, seasonings, honey & molasses in 5 gallon pot and bring to a boil.
Turn down and simmer 1 hour stirring occasionally.
Add processed veggies and kielbasa and return to a boil.
Simmer 15 min. or until beans are done.
Remove from heat.

Italian Barley Soup -Yield 3 gallons

3 Tbl. olive oil
3 onions diced
2 lbs. carrots sliced
1 bunch celery sliced
2 green peppers diced
6 qts. water
1 - 11 oz. box quick cooking barley
1 c. beef soup base
1/2 c. sweet basil
3 Tbl. oregano
1 t granulated garlic
1 t pepper
1 Tbl. sugar
2 c. tomato paste
1 #10 (102 oz.) can diced tomatoes
1/4 c. red wine vinegar

Brown onions in olive oil. Add carrots, celery, green peppers and sauté 20 min. stirring often. Next add all the rest of the ingredients and bring to a boil. Turn down and simmer 15 min. or until carrots are tender. Garnish with grated parmesan cheese. Before serving add 3 c Burgundy.
To make beef-barley soup, make beef stew meat on pg. 51 and adjust the liquids and seasonings.
.

Russian Borscht- yield 3 gallons

2 Tbl. butter
3 onions, diced
1 lb. carrots, sliced
1 bunch celery, sliced
6 qts. water
1 c. beef soup base
3 Tbl. dill weed
1 t granulated garlic
1 t pepper
1/4 c. red wine vinegar
2 Tbl. sugar
5- 16 oz. cans sliced beets or
6 lbs fresh beets cooked & sliced
4 lbs. cabbage cubed

Brown onions in butter. Add carrots & celery and sauté 10-15 min. until fragrant. Add water and seasonings and bring to a boil. Turn down and simmer until carrots are barely tender. Next add cabbage to the soup and bring back to a boil. Turn down and simmer 5 min.
Last, add beets and juice and remove from heat. Serve with a dollop of sour cream and a sprinkle of parsley.

Chicken or Turkey & Dumpling Soup - yield 3 gallons

2 Tbl butter
2 onions diced
2 lbs carrots sliced
2 bunches celery sliced
1 green pepper diced
6 qts water
1 c chicken soup base
(1 t Magic seasoning opt) *
1 t pepper
1 bunch parsley minced
3 lbs cooked turkey or
chicken cubed

Dumplings

7 eggs
2 c flour
1 t salt
mix together with a fork

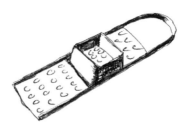

Lightly brown onions. Add carrots, celery and green pepper and sauté about 8 min. Add water and seasonings. Bring to a boil and simmer for 5 min. Turn up heat and make dumplings right into the soup by plopping in teaspoonsful of batter, or use a dumpling maker. Last add chicken or turkey and bring back to a boil. Remove from heat and add parsley. Divide and chill.

*Paul Prudhomme's poultry Magic

Split Pea Soup - yield 3 gallons

5 lbs split peas

| 3 lg onions |
| 1 bunch celery | >>> process until fine
| 2 lbs carrots |

1 t granulated garlic

2-3 bay leaves

1 t pepper

4 Tbl sugar

1 t ground sage

1 t Italian herbs

1/2 c ham soup base

3 lbs ham cubed

2 gallons water

Put peas and water in a pot and bring to a boil. Add everything else, turn down and simmer 30 min. Taste.

German Lentil Soup with Sausage - yield 3 gallons

4 lbs brown lentils

| 3 onions |
| 1 bunch celery | >>>process until fine
| 2 lbs carrots |

1 t granulated garlic
2-3 bay leaves
1 t pepper
1/2 t ground cloves
1 Tbl sugar
1 t mixed herbs (Italian)
1 c ham soup base
2 gallons water
1/2 c red wine vinegar
3-4 lbs smokie links sliced

Put lentils and water in a pot and bring
to a boil. Add everything except smokie
links and return to a boil. Turn down
and simmer 20 min or until lentils are
tender. Last add smoked sausage and
remove from heat. Divide and chill.

<u>Wisconsin</u> <u>Cheese</u> <u>Soup</u> - yield 3 gallons

2 onions diced
2 lbs carrots sliced
1 bunch celery sliced
2 gallons water
1 c chicken soup base
1/2 c dijon mustard
1 t pepper
4 c shredded swiss cheese mixed with 2Tbl cornstarch
4 c shredded cheddar cheese
2 lbs sliced American cheese
1 qt heavy cream

Roux = 2 c butter, 2 c flour cooked together 10 min and set aside.
Lightly brown onions in some butter, then add carrots and celery and sauté 5 min. Pour in water, add seasonings and bring up to a boil. Turn down and simmer 5 min, Add the cheeses slowly, stirring constantly. When the cheeses are all melted, add the hot roux and stir until thickened. Remove from heat and stir in the cream.
Taste, then divide and chill.

Pizza Soup - yield 3 gallons

4 onions diced
3 Tbl olive oil
3 green peppers diced
1 lb mushrooms sliced
1 #10 can (102 oz) spaghetti sauce
1 #10 can (102 oz) diced tomatoes
1 #10 can (102 oz) water
3 lbs cooked (hot) Italian sausage chopped
1 lb shell noodles cooked
3/4 c beef soup base
2 T sugar
1 t granulated garlic
1 Tbl sweet basil
1 Tbl oregano
1/2 t fennel seed

Brown onions in olive oil. Add green peppers and mush-rooms and sauté 5 min. Pour in spaghetti sauce, tomatoes, water and seasonings and bring to a boil. Tun down and simmer 5 min. Last add cooked Italian sausage and remove from heat. Add cooked noodles just before serving.

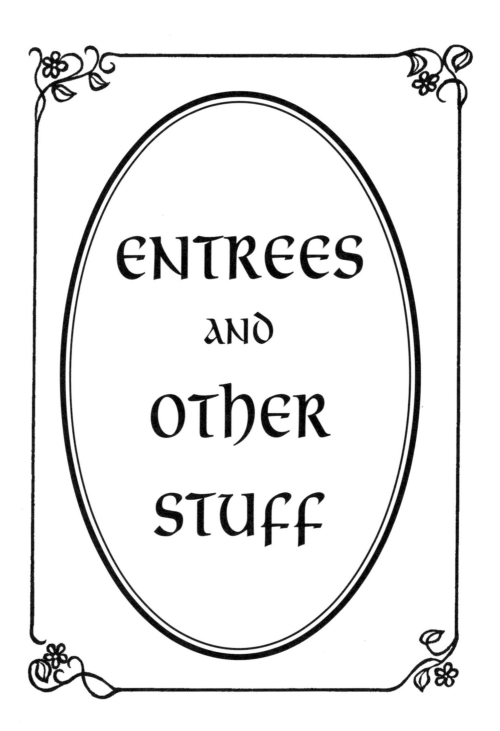

ENTREES

AND

OTHER

STUFF

Spinach Lasagna - yield 2- 9x13 pans or 20 servings

1 #10 can (102 oz) spaghetti sauce
2 - 15 oz pkgs ricotta cheese
6 pkgs chopped spinach thawed (or 2 lbs fresh baby spinach)
1 1/2 c grated parmesan/romano cheese
3 lbs shredded mozzarella
8 sheets frozen pasta

Mix ricotta with 1/2 c sour cream, 1 t granulated garlic,
2 Tbl dry basil, 1 Tbl seasoning salt.
Squeeze the water out of the spinach.
Put a thin layer of sauce on the bottoms of 2 9x13 pans.
Now layer:
>   noodles
>   sauce
>   parmesan/romano
>   mozzarella
>   spinach

>   noodles
>   sauce
>   ricotta mixture
>   parmesan/romano
>   spinach
>   mozzarella

>   noodles
>   sauce
>   mozzarella

Bake @ 325' for 1 1/2hrs on the bottom shelf. Cover with foil
that you have sprayed with Pam and let rest 1/2 hr before
cutting in 10 pieces. Serve with Italian bruschetta, page 36.

<u>Italian</u> <u>Bruschetta:</u>

20 pieces of bread
3/4 lb butter
2 Tbl basil
1 Tbl oregano
1 t granulated garlic

Melt butter in microwave then add seasoning. Paint bread slices and bake @ 425' 10 min. Rotate pans and keep baking until brown and toasty.

Spanish Rice - yield 4-5 qts.

8 c cooked rice (**not** minute rice)
3 Tbl olive oil
4 onions - lg dice
4 gr peppers - lg dice
1 -#10 can (102 oz) diced tomatoes
1 c tomato paste
1 t granulated garlic
1 Tbl sugar
3 Tbl beef soup base diluted in 1/2 c
hot water
2 c salsa (med hot)

Brown onions in olive oil, Add peppers and cook a few minutes. Now add everything else and stir. Divide and refrigerate. Or, to serve immediately, heat through.

<u>Southwestern</u> <u>Omelette</u> <u>or</u> <u>Burrito</u> - yield 20-24 servings

6 cans (15oz) black beans with cumin and chili spices
(Kuner's brand)
2 lg white onions finely diced
1 Tbl minced garlic
2 bunches cilantro chopped
2- 4 oz cans diced jalapeños
2 limes - juice
1 bag (14 oz) tortilla chips crushed
4 lbs colby/jack cheese - shredded
4c sour cream
4 c salsa
Avocado slices

Mix black beans with onions, garlic, cilantro, jalapeños and
lime juice. Spoon into omelette and add some crushed tortilla chips and jack cheese. Place omelette under the broiler
until filling is heated and cheese is melted. Turn out
omelette and top with sour cream and salsa.
For burrito, spoon filling onto an 8 or 10 inch flour tortilla
and top with chips and cheese. Fold, roll and serve with
sour cream, salsa and avocado.

Roast Salmon with Risotto Primavera - yield 14 - 6oz servings of salmon

6 lbs salmon filets. Ask the butcher to skin them and cut them into 6 oz portions. Marinate the filets in:
2/3 c dry white wine
2/3 c apple or orange juice
2/3 c soy sauce

Let them marinate for 2 hours turning once. Then lift out shaking off excess liquid and place on two baking sheets "skin" side down. Preheat oven to 450 ' and roast salmon for 15 min. Remove from oven and serve with risotto primavera (on next page).

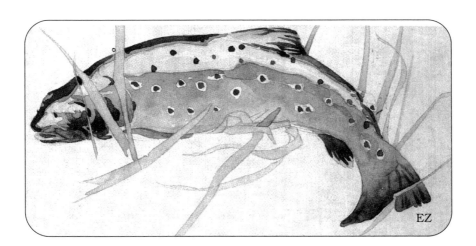

EZ

Risotto Primavera - yield 15 servings

Vegetables:
1 lb asparagus in 2"pieces
2 zucchini sliced
2 yellow squash sliced

2 lg white onions diced
6 tbl olive oil
23 oz pearl rice (3 1/2 c)
1 cup chablis (white wine)
2 cups sliced carrots
9-10 cups chicken broth - HOT

2 c frozen peas or fresh
1 cup thinly sliced fresh basil
1/4 lb cold butter sliced
1/2 c toasted almonds
2-3 c freshly grated parmesan

In a lg heavy skillet heat 3 Tbl olive oil and sauté the **vegetables** for a few min. until they just start to soften, set aside. Heat 3 Tbl olive oil in lg. pot. Add onion and sauté until softened, 3-4 min. Add rice, cook and stir 3-4 min. Add wine and simmer until absorbed stirring occasionally. Add 2 cups hot chicken broth and sliced carrots, simmer until almost absorbed. Keep on adding 2 cups broth and simmering until it's absorbed, about 15-20 min. Last add sautéed vegetables, peas, butter, basil, cheese, toasted almonds. Season with salt & pepper.

Quiche Lorraine - 3 - 9" pies

3 unbaked pie shells
12 oz cream cheese
12 eggs
4 c milk
2 t salt
1/4 t pepper
6 c grated swiss cheese
3 c chopped bacon
2 c caramelized onions

Put cream cheese in the food processor and cream. Slowly add eggs while continuing to process.
Scrape sides and add salt and pepper. Pour milk into a container and add egg mixture. Now fill the pie shells with onions, bacon and cheese. Pour the egg mixture over the top. Bake in a 325 ' oven on the bottom shelf for 1 1/4 hrs or until done.

Batter for 1 Quiche
4 oz cream cheese
4 eggs
1 1/3 c milk
3/4 t salt
1/8 t pepper

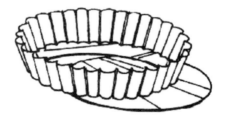

Brie and Walnut Quesadillas - 16 servings

Candied maple walnuts:
2 cups walnut halves
4 Tbls maple syrup
Toss nuts and syrup in a bowl.. Spread on a foil lined sheet pan and bake at 350 for 18-20 min stirring occasionally. Can be made days ahead.

Quesadillas

16 - 10" flour tortillas
2 lbs. Brie in 1/2" slices
1 bunch cilantro - tops
2 c candied walnuts
1 c soft butter

Butter tortillas on one side. Put buttered side down and cover half the tortilla with cheese nuts and cilantro. Fold in half and place on sheet pan. Can be made ahead. When ready to cook, place on hot grill and cook 1 min per side until brown on the outside and melted on the inside. Cut into 3 wedges and serve.

✻   **✻**

Other fillings for Quesadillas:

Pesto, shredded chicken, tomatoes and cheese or ...

Fresh spinach, fresh parmesan/romano cheese, portabello mushrooms, tomatoes and mozzerella or ...

Rice, seasoned black beans, roasted corn, cilantro and Colby/Jack cheese. Serve with sour cream.

Veggie Pita Pizza - 20 servings

20 Greek Flat Breads
2 - 1 lb pkgs broccoli flowers steamed 2 min
2 green peppers diced
2 bunches green onions finely sliced
2 - 1 lb pkgs grape tomatoes halved
1 lb sliced mushrooms
2 lbs shredded mozzarella & cheddar mixed
8 oz grated parmesan/romano/asiago mixed

Mix the following:
1 qt Hellman's Mayonnaise
1 Tbl dill weed
2 t Coleman's dry mustard
1 t granulated garlic
2 Tbl sugar

Spread pita bread with mayonnaise mixture and then top
with vegetables and cheese. Bake on grill for 1 min. then put
under the broiler for another min. Cut in quarters and serve.

Oriental Omelette with Brown Sauce - yield 20 servings

Omelette filling:
5 lbs cooked shrimp
4 lbs mung bean sprouts
1 c chopped green onions
3 cans sliced water chestnuts (save the juice for sauce)
1 bag toasted chinese noodles

Brown Sauce:
juice from 3 cans of water chestnuts
1 cup soy sauce
2 qts water
1 t granulated garlic
1 c cornstarch dissolved in 1 c cold water
Bring first 4 ingredients to a boil. Add dissolved cornstarch and whisk until thickened.

Top omelette with brown sauce and toasted chinese noodles. This recipe can be used for Egg Foo Yung.

Albacore Pasta Salad - yield - 24 servings

1 can (48 oz) Albacore Tuna, drained and shredded
2 lbs green peas (fresh or frozen)
3 carrots sliced
1/2 bunch celery sliced
1 green pepper diced
1/4 head red cabbage diced
1 bunch green onions sliced
5-6 lbs cooked pasta (rotini or penne etc)
10 hard eggs, sliced
6 tomatoes (or grape tomatoes)
2 c black olives halved
1 bunch parsley tops minced

Dressing:

4 c mayonnaise
2 c salsa
1 Tbl dill weed
1 t granulated garlic
1/3 c fresh lemon juice (2 lemons)
1 Tbl Worcestershire sauce
1 16 oz jar sweet pickle relish
3 Tbl Dijon mustard
1 t black pepper
1 Tbl seasoning salt
2 Tbl sugar

Garnish:

Tomato wedges
black olives
sliced hard egg
parsley, chopped

Mix pasta, tuna, and vegetables with dressing and serve
1 1/2 cups on a bed of chopped lettuce. Apply garnishes.
Voila!

Joe's Special - yield - 6 quarts

5 lbs ground beef
1/2 c flour
3 Tbl olive oil
6 onions diced
3 lbs mushrooms sliced
6 - 10 oz pkg chopped spinach - squeezed
3 Tbl beef soup base diluted in 1/3 c water
1/2 t nutmeg
1 t pepper
1/2 t oregano
1/2 t basil
1 t granulated garlic
5 eggs

Brown onions in olive oil and set aside. Brown ground beef and add 1/2 c flour and set aside. Now sauté mushrooms and set aside. In a large pot, cook spinach in 3 Tbl olive oil for 6 min. Then add diluted beef base and seasonings. Add onions, beef and mushrooms and heat. Last add eggs and cook and stir until just done. Serve in an omelette, over rice or in pita bread.

<u>Greek</u> <u>Feta</u> <u>Omelette</u> - filling for about 12-15 omelettes

2 Tbl olive oil
3 pkgs chopped spinach thawed and drained
2 onions diced
1 Tbl Basil
1 t oregano
1/4 t granulated garlic
1/2 t salt
2 c ricotta cheese
1/2 c parmesan/romano cheese
16 oz feta cheese crumbled
2 lbs mozzarella

In a lg fry pan sauté onions in olive oil. Add spinach and
cook about 5 min. Add basil, garlic and salt.
Cook another 3-4 min.. Cool mixture and add ricotta,
parmesan/romano and feta cheese. Use as filling for
omelettes along with mozzarella. To make sure the filling is
hot and the cheese is melted put omelette under a broiler for
about 30 seconds.

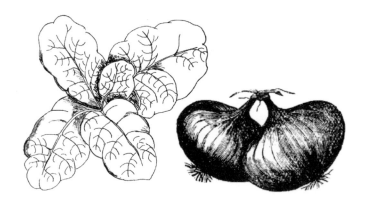

Festive Turkey Sandwich - 18 servings

1 1/2 lbs cream cheese
4 c frozen or fresh cranberries
1 small orange
3/4 c sugar
(1/4 t xanthan gum)

7 granny smith apples peeled and sliced (soak in water and
lemon juice or Fruit Fresh)
5 lbs sliced turkey
36 slices cooked bacon
36 slices bread

Put cranberries and cut up orange in food processor and
chop. Remove and put in a bowl. Next put sugar and cream
cheese in processor and mix. Remove and stir into cranberries.
Toast bread, spread with cranberry mixture, Add 4 oz grilled
turkey, 3-4 slices of apple & 2 slices of crisp bacon.

.

Enchilada Casserole - yield four 9x13 pans

6 lbs ground beef
4 lg onions diced
6 pkgs. Taco mix (or approx 3/4 c)
1 c flour
1 1/2 t granulated garlic
1/4 c sugar
1 Tbl ground cumin
1/2 t cinnamon
1/2 t ground cloves
2 - 12 oz cans tomato paste
1 #10 (102 oz) can diced tomatoes
1/4 c red wine vinegar
2 c water
3 - 4 oz cans chopped green chilies
1 - 4 oz can diced jalapeños
4 c chopped olives
2 lbs shredded Jack cheese
2 lbs shredded cheddar
2 c chopped green onions
4 doz corn tortillas cut in half

Brown onions and hamburger. Add all dry ingredients and cook a few min. Then add tomato paste, tomatoes, vinegar, water and simmer 5 min. Remove from heat. Now assemble casserole in 3 layers - Tortilla halves, meat sauce, jack cheese. green chilies & jalapenos.. -next layer -tortillas, meat sauce, cheddar. -last layer - tortillas, meat sauce, olives. green onions and top with a little cheese. Bake @ 350 ' for 1 1/2hrs. Let stand 1/2 hr before cutting.

49

Biscuits & Gravy - yield approx 1 gal

Biscuits: 20 - 2"
4 c flour
2 Tbl sugar
2 Tbl baking powder
1/2 t baking soda
1 t salt
1 c cold butter sliced
4 eggs
1 1/4 c buttermilk
Put first 5 ingredients in the food processor and mix. Next
add sliced butter and mix until fine. Now all at once add
eggs and buttermilk and pulse until barely mixed. Remove
dough to a floured board and knead 10 times. Pat and roll to
1/2 " thick. Cut out biscuits and bake @425' 15 min.

Sausage gravy: - 4 qts
5 lbs Jimmy Dean sausage browned and set aside
make roux::

| 1 1/2 c butter | >>> cook 10 min on low heat and set aside |
| 1 1/2 c flour |

3 qts milk
2 c heavy cream
1 t poultry seasoning
3 Tbl chicken soup base
1 t curry powder (opt)
1 t black pepper
In a double boiler bring the rest of the ingredients up to a
simmer. Whisk in roux and stir until thickened. Add
sausage and serve over split Biscuits

Beef Stew - yield - 4 gallons

10 lbs tenderloin tips (or if **for soup**, round steak)
8 lg onions lg dice
2 - 12oz cans beer
1 c soy sauce
3 bay leaves
1 t granulated garlic
1/2 c beef soup base
1 t black pepper
1 - 12oz can tomato paste
1 Tbl sugar
6 c water

Vegetables:
10 lbs potatoes peeled and cubed
4 lbs carrots peeled and cut in 1" slices
2 bunches celery in 1 " slices
2 green peppers 1" dice
1 lb frozen peas
1 lb frozen corn
1 lb green beans
1 lb lima beans

Coat meat with flour. Place on a well oiled sheet pan and brown in 450' oven for about 25 min.. Brown onions in a large pot. Add beef and the rest of seasonings and water. Cover and simmer about 45 min. Cook vegetables separately in 2 gallons boiling salted water (2 Tbl salt). Start with carrots, and bring back to a boil. Then celery, and potatoes and bring back to a boil. Last green peppers, lima beans, beans, peas, corn. Cook until just barely tender about 5 min. Drain liquid from vegetables into a container. Add vegetables to beef and add enough vegetable broth to make a nice stew.

Beef Pot Roast

8-10lb sirloin roast
2 - 12 oz cans beer
1/2 c soy sauce
1/4 c beef soup base
2-3 bay leaves
1 t granulated garlic
1 t pepper
4 c water
1 - 12 oz can tomato paste
1 Tbl sugar

Brown meat and add everything else. Simmer 3-31/2 hrs turning over once. Remove the beef and skim the fat off the remaining liquid. To make the gravy, bring the liquid to a boil, turn down and thicken with a roux.

Roux:
1 c butter
1 c flour
cook together 10 min on low heat
Slice beef and serve with mashed potatoes and gravy.

Dark Rye Bread - yield 16 - 2 pound loaves

5 lbs King Arthur rye blend flour*
1 lb pkg King Arthur rye bread improver*
6 lbs white flour
6 lbs fine grind wheat flour
2 c gluten flour
1/2 c dry yeast
1 c ground caraway seed
1/2 c dry dill weed
1 c cocoa powder
2 c sugar
1/2 c salt

2 tbl brown caramel food color
2 c dark molasses
2 c vegetable oil
4 12 oz cans beer - warm & flat
4 1/2 qts warm water (110')

caraway

Mix all dry ingredients together in a large tub and make a well in the middle big enough to hold 2 cups of liquid. Get 2 cups warm water (110') add a pinch of sugar and 1/2 cup yeast. Stir and let proof 3 min. Now pour yeast mixture into well and stir in a little flour at a time until you have a paste. Cover up the paste with flour and let rise 15 min. Have all the liquid ingredients warm, then add them all at once. Now dive in with both hands and stir around (like making mud pies). Get dough into a big blob, turn out onto a floured surface and knead 10 min. Put dough back into tub to rise for about 1 hr. covered with a towel. Punch back and let rise a second time, about 30-40 min. Now turn out dough and cut into 2 lb lumps. Shape into loaves and put in 5x10"pans to rise again about 45 min Bake @ 350' 48 min. Take out 8 loaves in back and bake front ones 13 min more.
Bread freezes very well.
*The Baker's Catalogue

"MD" or Whole Wheat Bread - yield 16 - 2 pound loaves

12lbs whole wheat flour- finely ground
6 lbs white flour
2 cups gluten
1/2 cup salt
2 c water @ 110 degrees
pinch sugar
1/2 c instant dry yeast (saf brand)
1 c blackstrap molasses
1 c honey
2 c corn oil
5 1/2 qts warm water (110 ')

Mix wheat & white flours and gluten in large tub. Pour 1/2 c salt around the perimeter. Make a well in the middle big enough to hold 2 c liquid. In 2 c warm water, mix pinch of sugar and the yeast and let stand 3 min. Now pour yeast mixture into the well. Stir in some flour to make a paste, then cover the paste with flour and let rise 15 min.
Now add molasses, honey, oil and warm water. Dive in and slosh around until you have a sticky mass. Work in the flour from the bottom and try to make a big rough ball. Turn out onto floured surface and knead for at least 10 min. Put back in tub to rise for about 1 hour or until double in size, Punch back and let rise again for about 1/2 hr. Turn out dough and cut into 16 - 2 lb blobs. Shape and place in 5"x10" pans.

Put in a warm place (gas oven with pilot light) to rise again for about 45 min.. Turn on ovens to 350 'and bake for 45 min. Take out the 8 loaves in back and put the front ones back in for another 13 min. Turn loaves out onto cooling racks for 1 hour. Bag and freeze.

<u>Meg</u> <u>Bread</u> <u>or</u> <u>White</u> <u>Bread</u> -yield 16-loaves (1lb 14oz each)

18 lbs white flour
1 c gluten
2 c sugar
1/2 c salt
2 c warm water @ 110'
pinch sugar
1/2 c instant dry yeast (Saf)
2 c corn oil
5 qts warm water @ 110'

Mix flour and gluten together. Put the salt and then the sugar around the perimeter. Make a well in the middle big enough to hold 2 cups liquid. In 2 c warm water mix pinch of sugar and the yeast. Stir & let sit 3 min. then pour into the well in the flour. Stir to make a paste. Cover the paste with flour and let rise 15 min. Now add the oil and 5 qts warm water. Plunge in and slosh around until you have a big sticky mass. Work in the flour from the bottom of the tub and try to get a big blob.

Turn out onto a floured surface and knead at least 10 min. Return dough to tub and let rise 1 hour or until double in size. Punch back and let rise again for about 1/2 hour.

Turn out onto floured surface and cut into 16 lumps of 1 lb 14 oz each.

Shape and place into 5"x10" pans and put in a warm place (gas oven with pilot light) to rise for about 40 min. Turn on oven to 350" and bake 40 min. Take out back loaves and replace front ones to bake for an additional 10 min. Cool for 1 hour, bag and freeze.

Oat Cakes - 4 quarts batter

4 c old-fashioned oatmeal 2 c flour 2 c whole wheat flour 1 1/2 t salt 2 Tbl baking powder 3 Tbl sugar	>>>Dry Mix

6 eggs 6 c milk	>>>Wet mix

1/2 lb butter melted

Mix eggs and milk in a large container. Add dry mix and stir until just barely mixed. Last add melted butter all at once and stir. Let batter sit 2 hours or overnight before using. Make pancakes as usual.

Corn Cakes- 4 qts batter

2 c cornmeal 4 c flour 1 Tbl baking powder 1 Tbl baking soda 1 t salt 1/2 c sugar	>>>Dry Mix

6 eggs 1 c buttermilk 4 c milk	>>>Wet Mix

1/2 lb butter melted

Mix eggs and milks together and then add the dry mix. Last add melted butter and stir. Let batter rest 2-3 hours or overnight. Make pancakes as usual.

Lloie's Salsa - yield 5 quarts

4 lbs Roma tomatoes
2 lg white onions
2 bunches cilantro
4 limes - 1/2 c juice
12-14 jalapeños
3-4 habeneros
1-4 1/2oz jar minced garlic
1/3 c red wine vinegar
2 Tbl ground cumin
2 Tbl salt
1 c tomato paste
2 t sugar

In batches, using the food processor, do the tomatoes, onions and cilantro <u>stems</u>. Now put on gloves and cut the peppers. Take the seeds and membranes out of all the Habeneros. Take the seeds and membranes out of <u>half</u> the jalapeños and leave them in the rest. Now put the peppers and the rest of the ingredients in the processor and run until it all becomes a paste. Add to tomato mixture. Mince the cilantro leaves by hand and stir into salsa. Wash food processor in <u>cold</u> water as this salsa is <u>extremely</u> <u>potent</u>, especially when fresh.

Chicken & Wild Rice Salad - yield 24 servings

24 - 6 oz skinless, boneless chicken breasts - pounded
1 - 36oz pkg Uncle Ben's Wild rice blend cooked
2 red peppers diced
2 green peppers diced
2 lemons - juice of
1 bunch cilantro minced
1 white onion finely diced
8 c red or green grapes

Dressing:
4 c mayonnaise
3 c med hot salsa
1 16 oz jar sweet relish
1 Tbl minced garlic
1 t Tabasco

Garnishes:
3 c toasted almonds
1 c black olives halved
salad makings, pg 61 (carrots, celery, green pepper, red cabbage)

Mix together wild rice, peppers. lemon juice, cilantro, onion, grapes and toss with dressing. Grill the chicken and cut into bite sized pieces. Place 1 cup of wild rice salad on a bed of chopped lettuce.Top with grilled chicken and garnish with salad makings,toasted almonds & black olives.

Chinese Chicken Salad - yield 24 servings

24 - 6 oz chicken breasts
10 pkgs Ramen Noodles (original)
3/4 lb butter
7 pkg Ramen Noodle seasoning
2 bunches bok choy
2 heads napa cabbage
1 lb snow peas
2 cans sliced water chestnuts
2 bunches green onions
2 red peppers
salad makings pg 61

Dressing
3 Tbl Poupon mustard
1 t granulated garlic
1/2 c red wine vinegar
1/2 c soy sauce
1 1/2 c sugar
4 c corn oil

Beat Ramen Noodles with a mallet until small and remove season pkgs. Melt butter. Fry noodles in butter until golden then stir in Ramen seasoning from **7** packets only.
Make dressing by putting everything except oil in the food processor. Start the machine and slowly add the oil. Keep running until the dressing thickens. Pound the chicken breasts with a mallet and refrigerate until ready to grill.
Cut bok choy and napa cabbage into bite sized pieces. Slice the red peppers finely for garnish. Slice the green onions. String and cut the pea pods. Slice & dice salad makings. Arrange salad on a plate. Now sprinkle chicken with seasoning salt and grill on both sides. Cut and place chicken on plated salad, top with toasted noodles and dressing.

<u>Greek</u> <u>Feta</u> <u>Salad</u> - yield 24 servings

5 lbs cooked pasta - rotini or penne or whatever
1/2 c olive oil
1 lb feta cheese crumbled
1 green pepper diced
1 red pepper diced
2 c green olives (or kalamata olives)
2 c black olives
2 lemons - juice of
1 lg white onion diced
1 Tbl dill weed

<u>Dressing</u>:
3 c Beulah dressing - see pg 75

<u>Garnishes:</u>
3 cucumbers sliced
3 pkgs grape tomatoes
24 lemon wedges

Toss pasta with 1/2 c olive oil. Add rest of salad ingredients and toss with 3 c Beulah dressing.
Place 2 cups salad on a bed of chopped lettuce and apply garnishes.

Mexican Pasta Salad - yield 24 servings

5 lbs cooked penne pasta
4 c halved grape tomatoes
10 ears roasted corn or 2 lbs frozen
1 lg white onion diced
2 cans (15 oz) Kuner's seasoned black beans
1 bunch cilantro chopped
1 - 4oz can diced jalapeños
8 c **salad makings:**
       1lb carrots sliced
       1 bunch celery sliced
       1 green pepper diced
       1/4 head red cabbage diced
6 heads leaf or romaine lettuce

Dressing
4 c mayonnaise
2 c salsa - med hot
1/3 c Dijon mustard
2 limes -1/3 c juice
1 t granulated garlic
1/4 c chili powder
3 Tbl ground cumin
1 Tbl seasoning salt
3 tbl sugar

Garnish;
8 c Salad makings
10-12 avocados sliced
4 c sour cream
3 c sliced black olives
4 c shredded cheddar cheese

Mix salad. Place 1 1/2 c on a bed of chopped lettuce and apply garnishes.

61

Pasta Salad Primavera - yield - 20 servings

5 lbs cooked penne pasta
4 c chopped ham **or** cooked cubed chicken breast
2 red peppers diced
3 lbs broccoli flowers, <u>lightly</u> steamed
2 c black olives
2 cups green olives
1 lg red or white onion diced
1 bunch green onions sliced
4 c salad makings:
(carrots, celery, gr pepper, red cabbage sliced,diced & mixed)
1 lb peas - fresh or frozen
2 c mixed parmesan/romano cheese
3 tbl chopped fresh basil
1 t fennel seed
4 c Beulah dressing (pg 75) mixed with 1 Tbl Tabasco
1/2 c olive oil
10 tomatoes wedged for garnish

Toss pasta with olive oil then add
everything else. Serve on a bed of
chopped lettuce and garnish with
tomatoes.

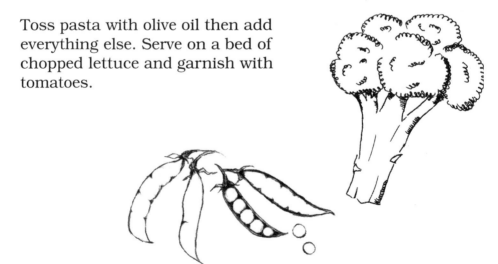

Salad Niçoise - approx 20 servings

4 lbs albacore tuna, drained and shredded
6 heads romaine or leaf lettuce in bite sized pieces
5 lbs small red potatoes, cooked and halved
5 lbs green beans halved and <u>lightly</u> cooked
8 c salad makings:
 1 lb carrots sliced
 1 bunch celery sliced
 1 green pepper diced
 1/4 to 1/2 red cabbage diced
10 hard eggs peeled and sliced
8 tomatoes cut in wedges
4 lemons cut in wedges
2 c lg black olives cut in half
6-8 c Beulah dressing (pg. 75) to be served on the side

Assemble the salad starting with the lettuce, salad makings, albacore. potatoes, beans, eggs, tomatoes, lemon wedge and black olives.

Taco Salad - yield 24 servings

10 lbs hamburger browned and drained
2 c taco seasoning mix
1 #10 can (102 oz) diced tomatoes
2 c salsa
2 c smashed taco chips (1- 13 1/2 oz bag)
1 t granulated garlic
2 Tbl ground cumin
2 c canned chopped green chilies
2 - 4oz cans diced jalapeños (opt)
3-4 white onions, diced in the food processor
1 bunch cilantro minced, stems and all
6-7 heads iceberg lettuce
Garnishes:
2 more bags (13 1/2 oz) tostitos
Tomato wedges or grape tomatoes
black olives
avocados (opt)
4 c sour cream
4 c shredded cheddar cheese

Brown meat, remove from heat and drain. Add taco mix stirring well. Now add tomatoes, salsa, smashed taco chips, garlic, cumin, green chilies, jalapenos, onions & cilantro.

Arrange salad in this order:
Chopped lettuce
6oz meat mixture
4 tomato wedges
8 tostitos standing up like a taco shell bowl around the meat
1 dollop sour cream
cheddar cheese
black olives
Avocado slices (optional)

<u>Chicken Normandy</u> - yield 24 servings -

24 - 6oz. skinless, boneless chicken breasts
1 - 13 oz. pkg. Rice Krispies
4 eggs
1/2 c. milk
3/4 lb. melted butter
dusting of pepper

Run Rice Krispies through the
blender until they are very fine, like flour.
Mix together eggs and milk. Dip chicken in egg-milk mixture
then in Rice Krispy flour. Place on foil covered pans. Paint
liberally with melted butter, and dust with pepper.
Bake in hot oven 450° for 15 min. Rotate pans and bake
another 10 min. or until nice and brown.
Remove from oven and top with

Sauce Normandy:
1 - 50 oz. can cream of mushroom soup
3 c. heavy cream
Mix and heat.

Serve over wild rice blend.
1 36 oz. pkg. (Uncle Ben's) wild rice blend

<u>Alaska</u> <u>Crab</u> <u>Sandwich</u> - yield 24 servings

3 lbs. cream cheese, softened
5 lbs. shredded crab, with legs (separated)
1 1/2 c. mayonnaise
3 Tbl. granulated onion
3 Tbl. dill weed
3 Tbl. chopped parsley
3 Tbl. lemon juice
2 t horseradish
1/2 t bouquet garni
1 Tbl. sugar
1/2 t Tabasco
1 t beaumond (opt.)
6 c. fresh bread crumbs
2-3 c. toasted almonds for garnish

Put cream cheese in food processor and mix. Add mayonnaise and seasonings, blending well. Place bread crumbs and shredded crab in a deep baking pan and stir in cream cheese mixture. Cover pan and bake 1 1/4 hours at 350° or until hot through.
Heat crab legs separately in a covered pan for 20 min.

To serve:
Grill a slice of bread until golden on one side. Spread crab mixture over untoasted side. Top with hot crab legs and toasted almonds.

Creôle Shrimp with Rice - yield 1-1/2 galions

6 lbs. cooked shrimp
1 c. butter
8 c. onions diced
3 c. green peppers diced
2 c. celery sliced
1/2 c. flour
2 t thyme
3 bay leaves
1/2 t cayenne pepper
1 t black pepper
1 Tbl. salt
2 Tbl. Worcestershire sauce
2 t Tabasco
2 c. dry vermouth
2 cans (1 lb. 12 oz.) diced tomatoes

Brown onions in butter.
Add green peppers and celery and sauté until tender.
Stir in flour and cook 5 min.
Then add everything except shrimp.
Stir and cook until mixture comes to a boil.
Turn down, add shrimp and cook until shrimp are hot.
Remove from heat and serve over rice, or in an omelette.

<u>Ratatouille</u>- yield 5 quarts

2 lbs. eggplant cubed
2 lbs. zucchini sliced
2 lbs. onions 1"dice
4 green peppers 1" dice
4 red peppers 1"dice
8 cloves garlic minced
4 lbs. canned diced tomatoes
12 oz. olive oil
1 c. chopped parsley
2 bay leaves
1/2 t thyme
salt & pepper to taste
Parmesan and Mozzerella cheese

Coat vegetables with olive oil and roast on baking sheets in a 450' oven 45 min. In a large pot sauté garlic in olive oil. Add tomatoes and seasonings and veggies. Bring to a boil stirring often and remove from heat.
To use for an omelette; put ratatouille inside and sprinkle with parmesan and Mozzerella cheese.
Fold omelette out onto a plate and top with more mozzarella.

Stroganoff - yield 3 gallons

10 lbs. ground chuck
1 gal. onions diced
1 c. flour
6 Tbl. sweet basil
2 Tbl. dill weed
5 Tbl. beef soup base - diluted in 1/2 c. hot water
2 t pepper
2 t granulated garlic
2 Tbl. Worcestershire
2 c. white wine (Chablis)
1 c. tomato paste
5 lbs. button mushrooms sliced
1 qt. sour cream

Brown onions and set aside. Sauté mushrooms and set aside. Brown ground beef and stir in 1 c. flour.
Add the rest of the dry ingredients. Stir in beef soup base, tomato paste,Worcestershire and white wine.
Add cooked onions and mushrooms and bring up to heat.
Last add sour cream.
Serve over wild rice blend and top with a dollop of sour cream and a sprinkle of paprika.

Verna's Sandwich - yield 15 servings -

1 1/2 lbs. cream cheese softened
48 oz. canned albacore tuna - drained
1 c. mayonnaise
2 Tbl. granulated onion
2 Tbl. dill weed
3 Tbl. chopped parsley
3 Tbl. lemon juice
1 t horseradish
1 t mixed herbs
1 Tbl sugar
1 t Tabasco
1 t seasoning salt
4 c. soft bread crumbs
sliced tomatoes

Place cream cheese in food processor and mix. Add mayonnaise and seasonings, blending well. Put albacore and bread crumbs in a deep baking pan and stir in cream cheese mixture. Bake covered at 350° for 1 1/4 hrs or until hot through.

To serve:
Grill a slice of bread on one side. Spread mixture on ungrilled side. Top with`sliced tomatoes and parsley.

Tørsk - yield 10 servings -

5 lbs. Icelandic cod filets
6-7 lbs. new red potatoes
2 gals. court bouillon
serve with melted butter & chopped parsley
Thaw fish in the refrigerato rovernight.
Cut into 8 oz. pieces. Bring court
bouillon to a boil.

Court Bouillon:
2 gals. water
1 c. lemon juice concentrate
1 c. red wine vinegar
1 onion sliced
1 lemon sliced
1/2 c. salt
1 tsp. peppercorns
2 bay leaves
1 bunch parsley stems
1/2 t thyme

>>>> Combine and bring to a boil. Then turn down and simmer 1/2 hr. Strain through a towel. Can be made the day before.

Plunge fish in and turn heat down to low. Cover and poach fish about 12 min.
Serve with boiled potatoes, melted butter and chopped parsley.

Tamale Torte - yield 4 - 9x13 pans -

Meat mixture:

10 lbs. ground beef

1 #10 (102 oz.) can diced tomatoes

4 onions diced

1 c taco seasoning mix

Wet Mix:	Dry Mix:
14 eggs	12 c. cornmeal
5 c sour cream	3 Tbl. baking powder
3 lbs thawed corn	1 Tbl. baking soda
1 28 oz can chopped gr chilies	1/4 c. sugar
2 lbs shredded cheddar cheese	1 Tbl. salt
1 c salsa	

Brown onions and set aside.

Brown hamburger and drain off excess fat and add taco seasoning, tomatoes and browned onions. Simmer 5 min. and remove from heat. Make wet mix by whisking eggs, then stir in all the rest of the wet ingredients. Mix dry ingredients together. Add wet mix to dry mix and fold in quickly. Divide 2/3 of the batter between 4 - 9x13 pans. Divide meat mixture equally, spooning it carefully over the batter. Dot with remaining 1/3 of the batter.

Bake at 350° for 1 1/4 hrs. Rotate pans after 45 min.

To serve top with chopped black olives and sour cream.

Warm Chicken Salad with
Orange/Rosemary Dressing - yield 24 servings -

24 - 6 oz. chicken breasts trimmed and flattened
Seasoned salt
3 c. craisins (dried cranberries)
24 white bread ends or slices
salad greens
salad makings (carrots, celery, gr pepper, red cabbage)

Grill chicken with seasoned salt about 5 min. on each side. Slice across the grain and lay on top of salad greens & vegetables. Top with some craisins and warm orange rosemary dressing. Garnish with black olives, orange slices and a slice of garlic toast.

Orange Rosemary Dressing: - yield 6 cups -

2 onions diced & browned in 1/2 c. butter. Add 1/2 c. flour & cook 5 min.

3 Tbl. grated orange rind
1 Tbl. ground rosemary
1 Tbl. salt
1 t pepper
1 t granulated garlic
*1 1/2 c. salad oil (added last - see below)

Then add the following:
4 c. orange juice
1 c. red wine vinegar
1/2 c. cranberry juice
1/3 c. sugar

Bring to a boil, turn down and simmer 3 min.
*Last, whisk in salad oil and serve warm with Garlic Toast on next page.

Garlic Toast: - yield 24 -

Seasoned butter:
Melt:
1 lb. butter
1 Tbl. dill weed
1/2 t granulated garlic

Brush bread with the above and place on cookie sheets.
Bake at 450° for 10 min. Turn pans and continue baking
until brown and crisp. Or place under the broiler.

Honey Mustard Dressing - yield 6 cups -

1/2 c. butter
2 onions diced
1/2 c. flour
4 c. orange juice
1 c. red wine vinegar
1 c. honey
1/2 c. country Dijon mustard
1 Tbl. salt
1 t pepper
1 t granulated garlic
1 Tbl. dill weed
1 1/2 c. corn oil - added last

Brown onions in butter. Add flour and cook 5 min.
Next add liquids and seasonings.
Bring to a boil, turn down and simmer 5 min.
Last whisk in corn oil and remove from heat.
Serve as a warm salad dressing.

74

Beulah's Salad Dressing - yield 1 gallon

1 c. country Dijon mustard
3 bunches parsley
1/4 c. granulated onion
1 c. concentrated lemon juice
3 c. red wine vinegar
2 1/4c. sugar
1/2 c. salt
2 Tbl. pepper
1 t granulated garlic
1 Tbl.Worcestershire
1 Tbl. dill weed
8 c. corn oil

Run all the ingredients through the blender in 3 batches, and combine in a gallon container.

Sauce Moreau, *or* creamy mustard sauce – yield 7 cups -

Roux = 1/4 c. butter & 1/4 c. flour
6 c. heavy cream
1/2 c. Grey Poupon mustard
1/2 t pepper

Make brown roux by cooking butter and flour together until a dark nutty brown. Heat cream and add seasonings. Whisk in roux, stirring until thickened. Served over grilled bread, ham and mushrooms it's "The Royal Stewart" sandwich.

Oma's Bread Stuffing - yield 1 - 9x13 pan -

2 gals. cubed stale bread
1/4 lb. butter
3 onions diced
3 stalks celery sliced
3 eggs
3 c. chicken stock
3 t sugar
3 t poultry seasoning
1 t ground rosemary
1 t pepper

Lightly brown onions in butter.
Add celery and sauté until tender.
Put bread cubes in a large bowl and
pour everything else on top, including
onions and celery.
Toss gently with hands until com-
bined.
Pile into a 9x13 pan, cover with foil
and bake in a 350° oven for 45 min.
Uncover and bake 15 min more

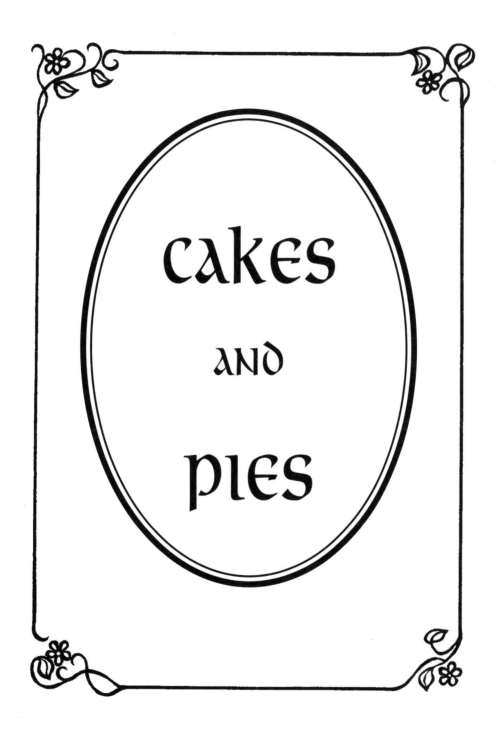

cakes

and

pies

Cranberry Nut Pie - yield 1 - 9" pie

1- unbaked 9" pie shell
1 1/2 sticks butter
2 c. cranberries
1/2 c. brown sugar
1/2 c. walnuts
2 eggs
3/4 c. white sugar
3/4 c. flour

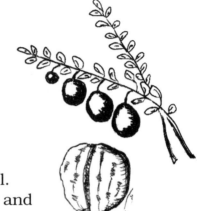

Melt butter and set aside to cool.
Layer cranberries, brown sugar and walnuts in the pie shell.
In the mixer, beat eggs with a whisk 5 min. at maximum speed.
Add white sugar and continue beating on high until light and thick.
Add cooled butter slowly, continuing to whip.
Last fold in flour with a spatula.
Pile mixture on top of cranberries and smooth out to the edges of the pie shell.
Bake at 350° for 50-60 min. or until brown and set in the middle.

Granny Smith Apple Pie - yield 2 - 9" pies

2 unbaked 9" pie shells
10 c. peeled sliced apples
1/2 c. butter/margarine
1 1/4 c. water
2 t vanilla
1 1/2 c. sugar
1 t cinnamon
6 Tbl. flour
1/4 t salt
1/2 t nutmeg

Cook apples, butter, water & vanilla in a covered pot until apples are barely tender.
Mix together dry ingredients and stir into apples. Keep cooking and stirring until mixture thickens.
Remove from heat. Pour into pie shells and top with

Streusel:
2 c. flour
2 sticks cold butter (1 c.)
1/2 c. sugar

Put everything in the food processor and run until mixture is very lumpy.
Sprinkle over apples. Bake at 425° for 30 min. or until bubbly and golden brown.

Banana Cake - yield 1- 9x13 pan -

1 1/2 c. butter/margarine mix
1 1/2 c. sugar
3 eggs
1 1/2 c. mashed bananas
2 1/2 c. flour
1 1/2 t baking powder
1/2 t salt
1 t vanilla

Cream butter & sugar. Beat in eggs,
bananas and vanilla.
Sift dry ingredients together and add.
Spread in buttered 9 x13 pan and add

Topping:
1 c. coarsely chopped walnuts
1 c. coconut
1 c. brown sugar
6 oz cold butter
1/2 c flour

Put all dry ingredients in a bowl. Slice in hard butter.
Work everything with fingers until blended and lumpy.
Sprinkle over cake batter.
Bake at 350° for 45 min. or until it tests done.
Cool and drizzle with thin powdered sugar icing.

Cheesecake - yield 1 - 9" cake

Crust:
1 c. flour
1/4 lb. cold butter
2 Tbl. sugar

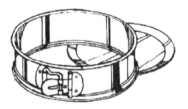

Filling:
1 1/2 lb. cream cheese
1 c. cottage cheese
1 c. sour cream
4 eggs
1 1/2 c. sugar
2 Tbl. lemon juice
1 t vanilla
3 Tbl. cornstarch

Topping:
2 c. sour cream
3 Tbl. sugar
1/2 t vanilla
          or
1 can raspberry
pie filling

Put crust ingredients into a food processor and run until lumpy. Press crust into a 9" springform pan. Go halfway up the sides and crumble lightly over the bottom.

Put all filling ingredients <u>except</u> <u>eggs</u> into food processor and run until smooth and creamy. Now add eggs and mix in quickly. Put filling into crust and bake at 350 °for 1 hr. or until set in the middle. Mix topping, and cover top of cheesecake.

Return to oven and bake for 10 min. Cool, then chill overnight before serving to achieve the best texture and flavor.

Carrot Cake - yield 1- 9" tube cake or 9x13 pan

4 eggs
1 1/4 c salad oil
2 c. sugar
1 t vanilla
1/2 t coconut extract
2 c. grated carrots
3/4 c raisins
3/4 c walnuts

2 c. flour
1 t baking powder
1 t baking soda
1 t salt
1 t nutmeg
1 t cinnamon

>>>sift

2 c grated carrots
3/4 c raisins
3/4 c toasted walnuts

Frosting:
4 oz. cream cheese
1/2 c butter/margarine
3 c powdered sugar
1/2 tsp vanilla

Beat eggs with whisk attachment until light and fluffy.
Add sugar. Then slowly add oil while beating on high. Add
vanilla and coconut extract. Change from whisk to paddle
and stir in dry mix on low speed.
Add carrots, raisins & nuts.
Pour into a buttered tube pan and bake at 350° for 1 hr. or
until it tests done.
Cool and spread with cream cheese frosting

Coffee Cakes - yield 3 - 8" square cakes

2 c. butter/margarine
3 c. sugar
9 eggs
6 c. flour
1 Tbl. baking powder
1 Tbl. baking soda
1 1/2 t salt
1 Tbl. vanilla
1 lemon - juice of
3 c. sour cream
2 c. chopped walnuts

Topping:
mix together:
1 1/2 c. brown sugar
1 1/2 t cinnamon
1 1/2 c. old fashioned oatmeal

Cream butter & sugar.
Add eggs one at a time.
Add lemon juice & vanilla.
Sift dry ingredients together and add alternately
with sour cream.
Divide batter into 3 buttered & floured 8" pans and
sprinkle with topping and chopped walnuts.
Bake at 360° for 45 min. or until they test done.

Custard Cups - yield 12- 5 oz. ramekins -

8 eggs
1 c. sugar
1/4 tsp. salt
4 c. milk
2 c. heavy cream
1 t vanilla
nutmeg, a sprinkle

Stir eggs until well blended.
Add everything except nutmeg
and stir well.
Place12 - 5 oz custard cups in two 9x13 pans with 2 c. water.
Fill custard cups, sprinkle with nutmeg and bake at 350° for
50 -55 min. or until barely set.
Remove from oven. Take cups out of baking pan.
Chill and serve.

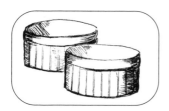

Apple Pike - 2 - 9" pies

1 c whipped butter/margarine (5 oz)
2 c sugar
2 eggs

1 1/2 c flour
2 t cinnamon
1/2 t nutmeg
1/2 t salt
1 t baking soda

>>>sift

1 c old-fashioned oats
8 c chopped granny smith apples

Cream butter & sugar. Add eggs one at a time. Sift dry ingredients. Add dry mix and chopped apples. Butter 2 - 9" pie plates thickly. Divide batter and smooth. Bake @ 350' for 1 hour on top shelf. Remove and glaze each with 3 tbls caramel sauce.

Caramel Sauce
1/2 c butter (1 stick)
1 c brown sugar
1/2 c heavy cream
2 Tbl corn syrup
1 t vanilla

Combine all ingredients, except vanilla, and boil 5 min. stirring occasionally. Remove from heat and stir in 1 t vanilla.
Serve with pike.

85

Amaretto Filling -

5 oz white chocolate melted & set aside to cool
1 c heavy cream with 1/4 c powdered sugar, whipped and
set aside.

Cream:
1/2 c whipped butter (2 1/2 ozs)
4 oz cream cheese
1/2 c sugar
2 egg yolks (stirred, heated and cooled)
3/4 t almond extract

Stir in white chocolate and whipped cream.
Split the layers and use this filling in a sponge cake (pg. 106)
or a chocolate cake, or fill a pie crust.
Toasted almonds are a nice addition.

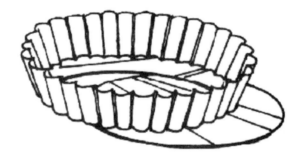

Bread Pudding - 9x13 pan

3 1/2 qts bread cubes poured into 9x13 pan

1 1/2 t cinnamon
1/2 t nutmeg
1/2 c brown sugar
3/4 c raisins

>>>mix and sprinkle over bread cubes

8 eggs
4 c milk
1 c heavy cream
2 t vanilla
1/2 t salt
3/4 c sugar

>>>mix and pour over bread cubes

1/2 c melted butter

Top with 1/2 c melted butter. Place pan on a sheet pan. Add
3 c water to sheet pan and bake @ 350' for 60-70 min. Cool
slightly and dust with powdered sugar.

Chocolate cheesecake - 1 - 9" cake -

Crust
1 1/2 c. chocolate cookie crumbs
3 Tbl sugar
pinch cinnamon (1/8 t)
1/4 c melted butter
mix and press into 9" springform pan.

Filling

8 oz <u>bittersweet</u> chocolate melted and cooled and added last
1 1/2 lbs cream cheese at room temp.
3 Tbl cocoa powder
1/2 c sour cream
1 tsp espresso powder
3 lg eggs
1 1/2 c sugar
1/4 t salt
2 t vanilla

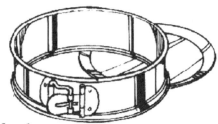

Put cream cheese and cocoa in food
processor and mix. Add sour cream, espresso powder, sugar,
salt, vanilla and mix. Next add chocolate. Last mix in eggs,
pour into crust and bake in a 350' oven for 1 hr or until set.
(*Opt. sour cream topping - 2 c sour cream, 2 Tbl sugar, 1/2
t vanilla. Return to oven and bake 10 min.)* Chill overnight.

Tip: Don't mix too long after eggs are added or cake will be
"poofy".

Cran/Apple Cream Pie - 1- 9"' pie

1 baked pie shell or crumb crust - 9"

1 c cranberries 1 apple - cored 1 Tbl lemon juice 3/4 c toasted walnuts or pecans 1/4 c brown sugar

>>> chop coarsely in food processor

8 oz cream cheese 1 pkg instant white chocolate pudding mix (3.3 oz) 1 c milk 2 c <u>whipped</u> cream 1/4 t xanthan gum

In a mixer, beat cream cheese until fluffy. Gradually add milk then pudding mix and xanthan gum. Fold in whipped cream and cran/apple mixture. Put filling in pie shell and chill 1-2 hours.

89

<u>Fresh</u> <u>Peach</u> <u>Pie</u> - 1 - 9" pie

Blanch peaches in boiling water for 30 sec before peeling.

6 c peaches peeled & sliced
1 unbaked pie shell
3 Tbl flour
1 egg
1/2 c sugar
1/3 c melted butter
1 t vanilla
pinch of salt

Place peaches in pie shell. Mix the other ingredients and pour over peaches. Bake in a 350 ' oven for 1 hour.

Fresh Strawberry Pie - 1 - 9" pie

1 baked pie shell
5 c fresh whole strawberries
1 c sugar
1/4 c cornstarch
1/4 c raspberry brandy
1/4 c water
1 t vanilla
1/4 t salt
1/4 t red food color

8 oz cream cheese
1/2 c sugar
1/2 t vanilla

Heat 2 cups berries in microwave for 2 min. Remove and mash them.

Mix brandy, water and cornstarch and add to berries. Now add 1 c sugar, salt, red color and vanilla. Return to microwave and bring carefully to a boil, stirring occasionally. Remove and set aside.

Mix cream cheese, vanilla and sugar in food processor. Spread it on the bottom of the pie shell. Arrange the rest of the berries on top of the cream cheese. Pour on the hot strawberry mixture and spread around carefully.
Chill for 1 hour.

Key Lime Pie - 1 - 9" pie

Crust
1 cup shortbread cookie crumbs
1 cup fresh bread crumbs
4 Tbl melted butter
2 Tbl sugar
Tear up a couple pieces of bread and process in the food processor. Add rest of ingredients and process a few seconds. Press into a pie plate and bake at 350' for 25 min. or until golden brown. Set aside to cool.

Filling
12 oz cream cheese
1 -15 oz can condensed milk
1/3 cup fresh lime juice (2 limes)
1/2 cup sour cream
green food color - a few drops
1/4 t xanthan gum
Put cream cheese in food processor and beat. Slowly add condensed milk, then lime juice, sour cream, xanthan gum, green food color and blend. Pour into baked crust and chill until set, about 2 hours. Serve with whipped cream.

Lemon Meringue Pie 1 - 9" pie

1 baked pie shell
grated rind from 2 lemons
juice from 2 lemons
4 egg yolks
1 c sugar
1 1/2 c water
1 t vanilla
4 Tbl cornstarch
pinch of salt
1/4 c butter

Combine and mix all ingredients in a 2 quart container and put in the microwave. Cook and stir until mixture comes to a boil. Remove and pour into a baked pie shell.

Meringue:
4 egg whites
pinch salt
1 t cream of tartar
1/2 c powdered sugar

In a mixer beat egg whites, cream of tarter and salt on high speed until foamy. Add powdered sugar and continue beating until stiff peaks form. Scoop meringue onto **hot** pie filling and spread it over the pie, sealing it to the crust. Bake in a 350' oven for 15-20 min or until golden brown on top. Cool slowly in a draft-free place.

93

Mrs Field's Chocolate Chip Cookies - yield 60 big or 120 sm.

8 oz whipped butter/margarine (about 1 1/2 c)
1 c brown sugar
1 c white sugar
2 eggs
1 t vanilla
2 c flour
2 1/2 c oat flour (put oatmeal in blender)
1 t baking soda
1 t baking powder
1/2 t salt
1 c chocolate chips
2 c toasted walnuts

Cream butter and sugar. Add eggs and vanilla. Sift dry
ingredients and add. Last add choc chips and nuts. Drop or
scoop onto cookie sheets and bake 12-15 min @ 375 '
depending on size. Do not over bake. Dough can be made
days ahead and refrigerated.

<u>Peach</u> <u>Cobbler</u> - yield 12- 5 oz ramekins

Blanch 10-14 peaches (in batches) in boiling water for 30 sec. each. Peel and slice.

<u>Biscuit</u> <u>Topping:</u>
2 c flour
4 Tbl sugar
1 Tbl baking powder
1/2 t salt
1/4 lb cold butter
2 eggs
1/2 c milk

Make biscuit topping in food processor. Put in flour, baking powder, sugar and salt and mix. Now cut in butter and stop. Put eggs and milk in and pulse until barely mixed.

<u>Peach</u> <u>filling:</u>
3/4 c water
1 Tbl lemon juice
1 c brown sugar
3 Tbl cornstarch
4 Tbl butter
1/2 t cinnamon
1 1/2 t vanilla
10 c sliced peaches

Stir and bring to a boil. Remove from heat and spoon 1/2 c peach filling into each ramekin. Put ramekins on a sheet pan. Plop biscuit mix on top of each in 2-3 mounds and bake on the top shelf @ 375 ' for 25 min.

<u>Peanut</u> <u>Butter</u> <u>Pie</u> - one - 9" pie

1 unbaked pie shell
4 eggs slightly beaten
1 c peanut butter
1/2 c honey
1/4 c butter - melted
1 t vanilla
1 c Karo syrup
1 c roasted peanuts

Mix everything <u>except</u> <u>peanuts</u> and pour into pie shell. Top with peanuts and bake at 350 ' for 50-60 min.

Raspberry Torte - one - 9"

Crust:
1 c flour
1/4 lb butter
1/4 c sugar

Topping:
3 pints fresh raspberries (1 pint is for top)
1/4 c water **or** raspberry brandy
1/4 c cornstarch
1 c sugar
1/4 t salt
1 t vanilla

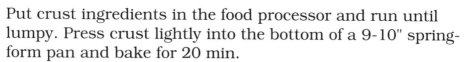

Filling
8 oz cream cheese
2 Tbl sugar
1 c heavy whipping cream
1/2 c powdered sugar
1 t vanilla

Put crust ingredients in the food processor and run until lumpy. Press crust lightly into the bottom of a 9-10" spring-form pan and bake for 20 min.

Place **2** pints of raspberries, cornstarch mixed with water **or** brandy, sugar and salt into a microwave-safe bowl and bring carefully to a boil stirring once or twice. Remove and stir in vanilla.

Now beat cream cheese with 2 Tbl sugar and 1 t vanilla. Whip heavy cream and powdered sugar until very stiff. Fold whipped cream into cream cheese mixture and place in cooled crust. Spread cooked raspberries on top of cream mixture and arrange last pint of raspberries on top.

<u>Rice pudding (Arroz con Leche)</u> - 12 - 5 oz ramekins

5 cups whole milk
1 cup condensed milk
1 cup evaporated milk
Combine milks and boil, stirring occasionally, until reduced
to approx. 3 cups, about 30-40 min.

Soak 2 cups pearl rice in 2 cups boiling water for 15 min.
then drain, rinse and reserve.

4 cups water
6 strips lemon peel 2"x 1/2" (grate the rest for garnish)
1/2 tsp salt
Bring water, lemon peel and salt to a boil. Add rice and bring
back to a boil.. Turn down and simmer 10 min. or until " al dente".
Discard lemon peel.

Stir in:
3/4 c raisins
2 t vanilla
2 Tbl sugar
3 c milk mixture - above
Spoon into ramekins and sprinkle <u>lightly</u> with cinnamon and
grated lemon peel.

Shortbread cookies - yield 1 10x15"pan

1 lb cold butter
4 c flour
1 c sugar

Put 1/2 the ingredients into the food processor and run until lumpy. Empty and process the other half. Knead together and press firmly into the pan Prick all over with a fork and bake @ 350 ' for 50 min or until barely brown. Cut into squares while still warm.

Walnut Shortbread Cookies
Prepare shortbread as above using an 11x17" pan and bake only 25 min.

Remove from oven and top with:
Walnut filling
4 eggs slightly beaten
1 c brown sugar
1 c Karo syrup
1/4 t maple extract
1/4 t salt
1/4 c melted butter
2 Tbl cornstarch
1 t vanilla
2 c (or more) walnuts
Return to oven and bake 30 min more @ 350 '. Cool slightly and cut into squares.

<u>Wild</u> <u>Blackberry</u> <u>Pie</u> - one 9" pie

Dough for 2 pie crusts
5 c blackberries

1 1/4 c sugar
3 Tbl tapioca flour
2 Tbl cornstarch
1/4 t salt
pinch cinnamon

>>>mix dry ingredients together

First put dry mix into the crust. Next pour in blackberries.

Top with a lattice crust, or a solid crust. Brush with beaten egg, and sprinkle lightly with sugar. Bake at 400 ' for 15 min, turn down to 350 ' and bake for another 50 min.

Meggie's Crunchy Granola - yield 1 1/2 gals. -

1 - 42 oz. box old fashioned oatmeal
2 c. wheat germ
1 1/2 c. brown sugar
4 c. sliced almonds
1 Tbl. salt

>>>Dry

1 1/2 c. corn oil
2/3 c. water
1 c. honey
1/2 c blackstrap molasses
1 Tbl. vanilla

>>>Wet

Mix dry ingredients together.
Mix wet ingredients together.
Combine wet & dry and mix well.
Spread 1/2" thick on 3 - 11x17 sheet pans.
Bake a 360° for 20 min. Rotate pans and bake 10 min. more.
Stir granola and return to oven for another 5 min. Continue
to stir and bake until a dark toasty brown.
Remove from oven and stir in:

2 c. raisins
4 c. toasted salted sunflower seeds
2 c. craisins (dry cranberries)

Cool and store in airtight containers.

101

Poppy Seed Torte - yield 2 - 9" layers -

Soak for 1 hour:
1 c. milk
1/3 cup poppy seeds

Cream:
1 c.whipped butter/marg (6oz)
1 1/2 c. sugar
Add 1 1/2 t vanilla

Sift together:
1 3/4 c. flour
2 1/2 t baking powder
1/4 t salt

Add dry and wet ingredients alternately to creamed mixture.
Beat 6 egg whites and fold into batter. Pour into 2 buttered,
floured 9" pans. Bake at 375° for 28 min. Cool 15 min.
before removing from pans. When cool, split layers and fill.

Filling:
1/2 c. sugar
2 Tbl. cornstarch
1 3/4 c. milk
6 egg yolks
1 t vanilla
pinch of salt

Combine and bring
carefully to a boil in the microwave, whisking twice. Remove
and whisk in 2 Tbls. butter/marg. Spread filling on first
layer and sprinkle with 1/3 c. chopped toasted walnuts. Fill
the next two layers and top with a dusting of powdered
sugar.

Pumpkin Pies - yield 2- 9" pies

2 unbaked pie shells
6 eggs beaten
1 can pumpkin (Libby's 29 oz.) or 4 c.
1 c. brown sugar
1/2 c. blackstrap molasses
1/2 c. sugar
2 t cinnamon
1 t ground ginger
1 t cloves
1 t nutmeg
1 t vanilla
1/4 t salt
2 c. milk
1 c. heavy cream

Paint pie shells with beaten egg
and allow to dry. Now mix ingredients and pour into pie
shells.
Bake 1 hour at 375° or until pie tests done.

Can also be poured into ramekins and baked. Serve with pie
crust triangles that have been painted with egg, sprinkled
with cinnamon- sugar and baked 25 min.

Pie Shells - yield 2 -

2 c. flour
6 oz. vegetable shortening
1 t salt
1 Tbl. sugar
1/2 c. ice water

Put flour, shortening, salt & sugar in food processor.
Run until crumbly. While still running, add cold water and
keep going until dough forms a ball.

Remove and divide ball in half to make two patties.
Wrap in plastic and chill.

Allow to soften slightly before rolling out.
Make lots and freeze.

Pumpkin Cake yield 1- 9 x13 or 1 tube pan -

2 c. sugar
4 eggs
2 c (Libby's) pumpkin
3/4 c melted butter - cooled
2 c flour
2 t baking powder
1 t baking soda
1/2 t salt
1 t ground ginger
1 t cinnamon
1/2 t cloves
1 t nutmeg
1 t vanilla
1 c toasted walnuts
1 c raisins

Beat eggs, then add sugar and continue beating until light.
Add cooled melted butter slowly continuing to beat on high.
Stir in pumpkin and vanilla. Fold in mixed dry ingredients,
walnuts and raisins.
Pour into buttered, floured tube or 9x13 pan. Bake at 350° -
50 min. or until cake tests done.

Frost with **Cream Cheese Frosting:**
4 oz. cream cheese
1/2 c. whipped butter/marg.
3 c. powdered sugar
1/2 tsp. vanilla

Strawberry Torte - yield 1 - 10" torte

4 c. whole fresh strawberries
1/4 c. cold water
1/4 c. raspberry brandy
1/4 c. cornstarch
1 c. sugar
1 t vanilla
a few drops red food color

Arrange 2 c. berries on the sponge cake. Heat the other 2 c. of berries in the microwave for 3 min then mash with a potato masher.
Stir water, brandy and cornstarch together and add with everything else to mashed berries. Now bring carefully to a boil in the microwave stirring twice. Pour over berries on sponge cake. Chill & serve with whipped cream.

Sponge Cake
3 eggs
1/2 c. sugar
1/2 c. flour
1/2 tsp. baking powder
1/4 t salt
1/2 t vanilla
1/2 t lemon juice

Beat eggs 5 min. Add sugar and continue to beat until thick. Add lemon juice and vanilla.
Mix dry ingredients and fold in by hand. Pour into buttered, floured 10" flan pan and bake at 375° for 19-20 min. Remove from pan and cool.

Swedish Apple Pies - yield 2 - 9" pies

2 unbaked 9" pie shells
9 c. sliced granny smith apples
4 Tbl. flour
2 c. sour cream
2 beaten eggs
1 t vanilla
1/4 t salt
1 1/2 c. sugar
1 lemon -grated rind & juice

Put sliced apples into 2 empty pie plates, cover with plastic-wrap & microwave 5 min. each.
Now put apples into unbaked pie shells.
Mix all other ingredients together and pour over pies.
Top with streusel.

Streusel:
2 c. flour
1/2 lb. cold butter sliced
1/2 c. sugar
1 t cinnamon

Put everything in the food processor and run until lumpy.
Sprinkle over pies.
Bake for 15 min at 400' then reduce heat to 375˚ and bake 40 min. more.

Walnut Pie - yield 1 - 9" pie -

1 unbaked 9" pie shell
4 eggs slightly beaten
1 c. brown sugar
1 c. light Karo syrup
1/4 t maple extract
1/4 t salt
1 t vanilla
1 Tbl cornstarch
1/4 c. melted butter
1 1/2 c. walnut pieces

Mix everything together and pour into unbaked pie shell. Bake at 375° for 55-60 min. or until the pie has risen and the middle is set.

French Chocolate Torte - yield 1 - 10" torte -

1 sponge cake - flan shaped (see pg. 106)
2 oz. bitter chocolate in 1/4 c water
1/2 c. whipped butter/marg.
4 oz. cream cheese
1 c. sugar
2 egg yolks
1/8 t rum extract **or** 1 t espresso powder
1 t vanilla
 pinch salt
1/4 c. powdered sugar
1 c. heavy whipping cream
semi-sweet choc. for garnish

Melt chocolate & water carfully in microwave and cool to
room temp - do not stir.

Cream butter, cream cheese & sugar.
Add egg yolks and beat well.
Add vanilla, rum extract **or** espresso powder, and salt.
Now stir melted chocolate until it thickens.
Add thickened chocolate and mix until smooth & creamy. In
a separate bowl beat whipping cream with powdered sugar
until stiff.

Fold whipped cream into chocolate mixture.
Pile it all onto the sponge cake and spread it out.
Top with shaved semi-sweet chocolate or drizzle with
melted bitter chocolate. Chill & serve.

Chocolate Cake - yield 2 - 9" layers -

3 oz. bitter chocolate
1/3 c. water
1 c. whipped butter/marg.
2 1/4 c. brown sugar
2 eggs
1 t vanilla
1 c. water
2 c. flour
1 t baking soda
1/2 t salt
1/2 t xanthan gum

Melt chocolate in 1/3 c. water and cool to room temp.
Butter 2 - 9" cake pans. Line bottoms with parchment
paper & dust with cocoa.
Cream butter & sugar. Add eggs & vanilla, beat well. Add
chocolate mixture.
Sift dry ingredients and add alternately with 1 cup water.
Bake at 350° for 30-35 min. or until cake tests done.
Cool 15 min. before removing from pans.
For a fancy cake, split the layers and fill with French
Chocolate on page 109. Drizzle 1/4 c raspberry brandy on
bottom layer. Dust finished cake with powdered sugar.

Cinnamon Rolls - yield 30 - 4oz. rolls -

| 1 c. hot (110°-115') water
3 Tbl. dry yeast
1 Tbl. sugar | >>>Dissolve and add to: |

1 c. flour. Stir and let stand about 5 min.
Then add:
3 eggs
1/2 c. corn oil
1/2 c melted butter
1 t vanilla
3 Tbl sweet dough flavor*
1 c. sugar
1 Tbl. salt
8 c. flour
4 Tbl dough relaxer*
3 1/2 c. hot (110°) water

Filling: use 1/2 for each piece
1 c. melted butter
2 c. brown sugar
1 c. raisins
1 Tbl. cinnamon
walnuts & raisins

Stir everything together.
Remove dough to well floured surface and knead a few min.
Place in oiled bowl to rise for 30-40 min.
Divide dough in half. Roll into a 30" by 20" rectangle.
Spread with 1/2 the filling and roll up firmly.
Cut into 15 pieces. Place cut side down on buttered sheet
pans and flatten slightly.

Let rise 40 min. then bake at 360° for 20 min.
Rotate pans and bake 10 min. more.
While still warm, paint with powdered sugar icing.
*The Baker's Catalogue

111

Rhubarb Pie - yield 2 - 9" pies -

2 unbaked pie shells
9 c. fresh rhubarb in 1/2" slices
4 Tbl.tapioca flour
2 Tbl. cornstarch
3 eggs, beaten
1/2 t salt
2 c. brown sugar
1/2 t nutmeg
2 t vanilla
1/2 c heavy cream

Paint pie shell bottoms with
beaten egg and let dry.
Cut rhubarb into 1" pieces and place in a bowl.
Add the rest of the ingredients and mix well.
Let the mixture sit 20-30 min. until it's soupy, then put it
into the pie shells and top with streusel.

Streusel:
2 c. flour
2 sticks cold butter
1/2 c. sugar

Put everything into the food processor and run until lumpy.
Sprinkle over the pies.
Bake at 375° for 1 hour until brown and bubbly.

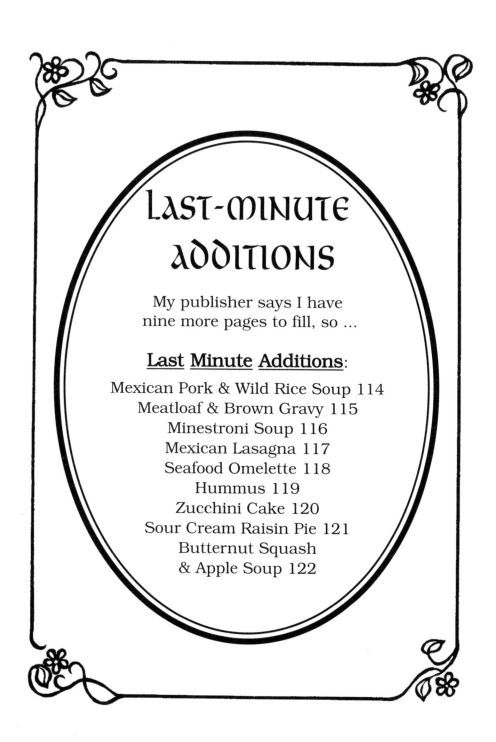

Last-Minute Additions

My publisher says I have
nine more pages to fill, so ...

THE KITCHEN TABLE

<u>Mexican</u> <u>Pork</u> & <u>Wild</u> <u>Rice</u> <u>Soup</u> - yield 2 1/2 gallons

6 lbs boneless pork steaks
2 lg onions diced
2 Tbl butter
1 t granulated garlic
3 - 15 oz cans garbanzo beans
3 - 15 oz cans great northern beans
1 - 26 oz can diced green chilies
3/4 c chicken soup base
4 qts water
2 Tbl ground cumin
1 t Tobasco
1/4 c lime juice
1 t black pepper
3 c <u>cooked</u> wild rice
1 bunch parsley chopped

Cook the wild rice.
Place the pork steaks on baking pans in a 450' oven, brown
for 40 min. Deglaze each pan with a cup of water and add to
soup. Cut the pork into 1/2" cubes and set aside. Next,
brown the onions in butter. Now add everything _except_ the
wild rice and bring to a boil. Simmer 10 min.
Add the cooked rice and divide into containers.

Meatloaf - yield 4 loaves or 28 servings

10 lbs hamburger
8 c soft bread crumbs
3 onions diced in food processor
10 eggs
2 Tbl salt
2 t pepper
2 Tbl Worcestershire Sauce
2 Tbl Pupon mustard

Mix lightly and divide into four pieces on two sheet pans. Shape into loaves and bake @ 375 for 1 hr.

Brown Gravy
Brown roux:
1 c butter
1 c flour
cook together until brown and set aside

To 2 qts boiling water add
3 Tbl beef soup base
1/2 c Burgundy
2 t brown color (Chinese Bead Molasses)
1/2 t ground rosemary
1/2 t pepper

Last add roux to boiling liquid and whisk briskly until thickened.

Minestroni - yield 3 gallons

3 Tbl olive oil
2 onions diced
2 lbs carrots sliced
1 bunch celery sliced
2 green peppers diced
1 bunch bok choy sliced
1 15 ox can kidney beans
1 15 oz can white beans
1 15 oz can garbanzo beans
6 qts water
1 c beef soup base
1/2 c sweet basil
3 Tbl oregano
1 t granulated garlic
1 t pepper
1 Tbl sugar
2 c tomato paste
1 #10 (102 oz) can diced tomatoes
2 c Burgundy
2 pkgs tortellini cooked
parmesan cheese to garnish

Brown onions in olive oil. Add carrots, celery, gr peppers and bok choy. Sauté 5 min stirring often. Next add water, tomatoes, paste, seasonings and bring to a boil. Turn down and simmer 8 min. Last add beans and wine and remove from heat. Divide into containers and chill.

Before serving add cooked tortellini and garnish with parmesan cheese.

Mexican Lasagna - yield 1- 9 x 13 pan

1 lb hamburger, cooked
2 cans (16 oz) refried beans
1 can (4 oz) jalapeños diced
2 t oregano
1 t ground cumin
1 t granulated garlic
1 pkg flour tortillas cut in half
3 c shredded cheddar cheese
2 c salsa

2 c sour cream
1 c green onions chopped
1 c black olives chopped

>>>topping

Combine hamburger, beans, seasonings, jalapeños & salsa. Place a layer of tortillas in the pan and spread on 1/2 hamburger mixture and 1/2 cheese.

Now make a second layer starting with tortillas, then meat and cheese. End with a layer of tortillas and spread on sour cream and sprinkle with onions and olives. Bake @ 350' for 40 min.

<u>Seafood</u> <u>Omelette</u> - yield 1 gallon

5 lbs cod
2 lbs lobster
2 lbs shrimp

>>> poach in court bouillon (pg 71)
for 12 min

1 c butter
1 c flour
1 1/2 qts milk
1 qt prepared hollandaise sauce
4 c Buttered bread crumbs

Make a roux by combining butter and flour and cooking for
10 min. Set aside.
Make hollandaise from pkg directions, set aside
Heat milk in a double boiler, add roux
and stir until thickened. Add hollandaise and seafood.

Make buttered bread crumbs by frying 4c soft bread crumbs
in 3/4 c butter until brown.

Use as filling for an omelette of serve over rice as an entrée.
Top with buttered bread crumbs.

Hummus - yield 1 quart

2 cans (15 oz) garbanzo beans
1/2 c tahini (ground sesame seeds)
1 lemon - juice of
1 Tbl ground cumin
1/2 t tabasco
1 t seasoning salt
1/2 t pepper
1/3 c water
1/4 c olive oil.

Combine everything in food processor and mix.

Mediterranean Special:
18 flat Pita breads
cucumbers
tomatoes - grape
black olives
chopped egg
parsley

Spread pitas with hummus and top with above ingredients.

Zucchini Cake - 1 tube pan

3 eggs
3/4 c oil
1 1/2 c sugar
1 t lemon rind or orange
1 t vanilla
2 c zucchini grated

2 1/2 c flour
1/2 t salt
1 t cinnamon
1 t ginger >>>sift together
1 t nutmeg
1 t baking powder
1 t baking soda

1/2 c toasted walnut pieces

Beat eggs 5 min with whisk attachment. Add oil <u>slowly</u>, then sugar. Switch to paddle attachment of mixer and add lemon, vanilla and zucchini. Mix in dry ingredients and nuts. Pour into a buttered tube pan and bake @ 350' for 55 min or until tester comes out clean.

Frosting:
4 oz cream cheese
1/2 c whipped butter/marg
3 c powdered sugar
1/2 t vanilla
grated orange rind or extract (opt)

Sour Cream Raisin Pie - one 9"

1 <u>baked</u> pie shell
2 c sour cream
1 3/4 c sugar
4 egg yolks
4 Tbl flour
1 3/4 c raisins
1/4 t salt
1 t vanilla
1/4 c melted butter

Mix everything <u>except</u> butter, Place in microwave oven and
bring carefully to a boil stirring often. Last stir in butter.
Pour into pie shell and top with meringue.

<u>Meringue:</u>
4 egg whites
1/4 t cream of tartar
1/2 c powdered sugar

Whip egg whites until frothy, add cream of tartar and sugar.
Now whip until stiff and spread on warm pie being careful to
seal meringue to the crust. Bake in a 350' oven for about 20
min or until lightly brown. Cool in a draftfree place.

Butternut Squash & Apple Soup - yield 3 gallons

6 Tbl butter
4 lg onions diced
12 lbs butternut squash peeled & cubed
4 qts water
1 c chicken soup base
4 apples peeled & sliced
2 c apple juice
1 t nutmeg
3 Tbl ground cardamom
juice & rind from a lemon
salt & pepper to taste

Brown onions. Add everything else & bring to a boil. Simmer
20-30 min or until tender. Puree and taste. Garnish with
toasted almonds.

The squash can also be roasted @ 450'
for about 40 min.

INDEX

Salads:
    Albacore Pasta 45
    Chicken, *with* Orange
     Rosemary Dressing 73
    Chicken & wild Rice 58
    Chicken, Chinese 59
    Greek Feta 60
    Mexican Pasta 61
    Niçoise 63
    Pasta Primavera 62
    Taco 64
Salad Dressing, Beulah 75
Salad Dressing, Honey
Mustard 74
Salmon, Roast 39
Salsa, Lloie's 57
Sandwichs:
    Alaska Crab 66
    Festive Turkey 48
    Verna's 70
Sauce Moreau 75
Shrimp, Creole With Rice 67
Spinach Lasagna 35
Spanish Rice 37
Tørsk 71
Tamale Torte 72

Cakes & Pies

Bread Pudding 87
Cakes:
    Banana 80
    Carrot 82
    Cheesecake 81
    Chocolate 110
    Pumpkin 105
    Chocolate Cheesecake 88

Cinnamon Rolls 111
Chocolate, French Torte 109
Coffee cakes 83
Cobbler, Peach 95
Cookies:
    Mrs Fields Chocolate-
    Chip 94
    Shortbread 99
    Walnut Shortbread 99
Custard cups 84
Granola, Meggie's Crunchy 101
Pies:
    Amaretto, Filling 86
    Apple, Granny Smith 79
    Apple, Pike 85
    Apple, Swedish 107
    Blackberry, Wild 100
    Cranberry/Apple Cream 89
    Cranberry/Nut 78
    Lime. Key 92
    Lemon Meringue 93
    Peach, Fresh 90
    Peanut Butter, 96
    Pumpkin 103
    Rhubarb 112
    Strawberry, Fresh 91
    Sour Cream Raisin Pie 121
    Walnut 108
Pie Shells 104
Poppy Seed Torte 102
Raspberry, Torte 97
Rice Pudding, Mexican 98
Strawberry Torte 106
Zucchini Cake 120